jennifer
cornbleet

raw food
MADE EASY
for 1 or 2 people
REVISED

Book Publishing Company
Summertown, Tennessee

Library of Congress Cataloging-in-Publication Data

Cornbleet, Jennifer, 1972-
    Raw food made easy for 1 or 2 people / Jennifer Cornbleet. — Rev. ed.
        p. cm.
    Includes index.
    ISBN 978-1-57067-273-6 (pbk.) — ISBN 978-1-57067-934-6 (e-book)
    1. Raw foods.   2. Cooking for one.   3. Cooking for two.   4. Cookbooks.   I. Title.
    TX392.C674 2012
    613.2'65—dc23

                                                                    2012004140

Cover and interior design: John Wincek
Cover and interior photos: Warren Jefferson
Food styling: Jennifer Cornbleet, Barbara Jefferson

Printed on recycled paper

BOOK
PUBLISHING
COMPANY

Book Publishing Company is a member of Green Press
Initiative. We chose to print this title on paper with 100%
postconsumer recycled content, processed without chlorine, which saved the following natural resources:

green
press
INITIATIVE

88 trees
40,280 gallons of water
8,932 pounds of greenhouse gases
36 million BTU of energy
2,553 pounds of solid waste

For more information on Green Press Initiative, visit
greenpressinitiative.org.

Environmental impact estimates were made using
the Environmental Defense Fund Paper Calculator
calculator.environmentalpaper.org/home.

Printed in the United States

Book Publishing Company
P.O. Box 99
Summertown, TN 38483
888-260-8458
bookpubco.com

ISBN: 978-1-57067-273-6

18 17 16 15 14 13 12   1 2 3 4 5 6 7 8 9

*Pictured on the front cover: Ramen, p. 87;
Pear and Parsley Green Smoothie, p. 49,
Blueberry Green Smoothie, p. 41, and
Honeydew Green Smoothie, p. 48; Black-
berry Crisp, p. 172, with Vanilla Ice
Cream, p. 191*

*Pictured on the back cover: Shaved Beet-
Salad, p. 110, Garden Wrap, p. 133,
Flourless Chocolate Cake, p. 162*

*Calculations for the nutritional analyses
in this book are rounded up to the near-
est gram. Optional ingredients are not
included, and if two or more options for an
ingredient are listed, the first one is used.
Since reliable data for most fresh fruit and
vegetable juices and nut and seed milks
are not available, nutritional analyses
for these recipes (and for recipes including these components) are based on the
whole-food ingredients, before juicing or
straining.*

CONTENTS

To my spiritual master and teacher,

Adi Da Samraj

Raw food has entered the mainstream—in popular diet books, casual and fine restaurants, cooking classes around the country, and food blogs across the Internet. And it makes sense. More people today are intent on staying healthy and are experimenting with eating less meat, less processed food, and more fruits and vegetables. Raw food fits perfectly into such an approach. People are also discovering that raw food is delicious and healthful and can be really, really easy to prepare. This is important at a time when we're all trying to fit twenty-five hours of living into a twenty-four-hour day.

So in this new edition of *Raw Food Made Easy for 1 or 2 People*, I've continued to offer tasty meals, snacks, and desserts made with basic equipment and everyday ingredients—and I've expanded the original to include what readers have asked for.

Just a few years ago, finding organic produce and natural ingredients was a challenge. But today many cities and towns have weekly farmers' markets with fresh-from-the-field produce. Specialty grocery stores, such as Whole Foods Market and Trader Joe's, carry lots of organic produce and products, and everyday supermarkets offer healthful ingredients such as flaxseeds, kale, miso, sprouts, and tahini. Organic suppliers online make it as easy as "point and click" to stock a raw-food pantry. As a result, I've been able to include new recipes that use a wider range of ingredients.

To help readers fit raw-food meals into diet plans, every recipe now includes nutritional information: calories, protein, fat, carbohydrate, fiber, and sodium. (Since reliable data for fresh juices and nut and seed milks are not available, nutritional analyses for these recipes are based on the whole-food ingredients, before juicing or straining.) It's important to note—raw dishes also provide abundant antioxidants, enzymes, and phytonutrients, which are not measured in the standard data. So count calories if you like, but know that raw recipes are good for you because they make every calorie count.

One addition I'm especially pleased with is the new chapter on green smoothies (see pages 37 to 50). These creamy and satisfying drinks are made from fresh fruits, leafy greens, and water. They pack a nutritional wallop along with outstanding flavor because dark green vegetables such as kale and collards are concentrated sources of protein, minerals, and phytonutrients. These drinks have become quite popular in recent years, but they still are not easy to find in juice bars or coffee shops. Fortunately, you can make them yourself!

In response to readers' requests, I've included more of the raw food recipes that we commonly incorporate into our diets—fruit dishes (see pages 28 to 36), salads (see pages 91 to 111), and salad dressings (see pages 113 to 123). I've also added tips for advance preparation (see pages 14 to 16). Prepping some food ahead of time is key to having nutritious meals ready during the week so you're never stuck wondering "What's for dinner?" (Or breakfast, or lunch, or midnight snack.)

To help people make good choices when they're eating between meals, I've included a section on easy snacks (see page 61). And in response to today's fast-paced lifestyle, I've also added a new chapter with tips for eating on the go and while traveling (see pages 154 to 156).

With all these additions, however, my approach to raw food still reflects my approach to life: keep it simple and enjoy! Whether you're just starting to add raw recipes to your culinary repertoire or are a long-term raw foodie, I'd like to help.

And I'd like to continue helping when you've finished reading *Raw Food Made Easy for 1 or 2 People*. Next Steps (see page 193) outlines several ways we can stay connected.

Best wishes for joy and good eating.

—*Jennifer Cornbleet*

ACKNOWLEDGMENTS

So many friends and students over the years have requested a book of simple, healthful, and delicious raw recipes. They wanted economical, practical, and quick-to-prepare food for one or two people. The dishes had to be familiar tasting and flexible, so that a variety of people, from raw-food enthusiasts to traditional diners, could enjoy them. I wrote *Raw Food Made Easy* in response to these desires. My gratitude to all of you.

My heartfelt thanks and appreciation to Keyvan Golestaneh, the holistic health practitioner who introduced me to the raw diet. Keyvan is a gifted healer. Working with him showed me the connection between my lifestyle and my physical and emotional health and helped me heal and become whole. I am blessed by his guidance, knowledge, wisdom, compassion, and healing on all levels.

Thanks to Nomi Shannon for teaching the first raw-food class I attended years ago. After that class, I knew I would teach raw-food classes someday.

My thanks to the staff of Living Light Culinary Arts Institute, including Cherie Soria, Dan Ladermann, David Ross, Patricia Hoskins, Alicia Ojeda, Martine Lussier, Gina Hudson, Colleen Cackowski, Terilynn Epperson, Karen Fraser, Kristin Suratt, Brenda Howard, Mellissa Sale, Barbara Howard, Rick and Karin Dina, and Julie Engfer. My years as a Living Light student and instructor have been filled with learning, growth, and good times.

Thanks also to Matt Samuelson and Elaina Love, two of the best raw-food chefs and instructors around. I've loved trading recipe ideas and working with you over the years.

I am also grateful to Cindy Schwimmer and her family for helping me test many of the recipes for this book and ensuring that they are kid friendly. Thanks especially to Cindy for her help with my Chicago classes. And thank you to my friend Bill Veeder, for rigorous editing and tasting so many of my recipes.

Thanks to the staff of the Book Publishing Company for all their flexibility and for making the editing, photography, and publishing process easy and fun.

Thanks to the marketing directors of Whole Foods Markets in Chicago, including Joyce Chacko, Kathy Kunzer, Victoria Reed, Sara Parenti, Megan Bowman, Troy Authement, and Elizabeth Boomer, and to Miranda McQuillan of Wild Oats Market, Marc Lapides of Northshore Cookery, Conery Hoffman of Sur La Table, and Karyn Calabrese of Karyn's Fresh Corner, for your commitment to promoting raw-food classes in Chicago. Your support has made it possible for me to share raw food with many people.

Many thanks to the following friends who generously allowed me to use or adapt their recipes for this book:

- Keyvan Golestaneh: Energizing-Purifying Juice (page 21), Fasting Juice (page 22), and Multiseed Porridge (page 54)
- Alissa Cohen: Garden Wrap (page 133) and Walnut-Raisin Cake (page 159)
- Elaina Love: Brownies (page 166)
- Matt Samuelson: Zucchini Hummus (page 70)

My most sincere thanks to my parents, Harry and Joanne Cornbleet, and especially to my mother for countless hours of work on my website.

Thank you, Mark, for being the most loving partner I could hope for. I feel so blessed to share my life with you.

Finally, I want to thank my assistants and students in Chicago, especially Connie Lambert, Carol Rodgers, Ellie Welton, Christina Taylor, Belinda Cusic, and Vanessa Sherwood, for inspiring me to teach about raw food and to write this book and for making it possible to teach so many classes.

A piece of juicy fruit, a crisp green salad, a handful of nuts . . . everyone knows how pleasurable and easy raw food can be. My goal is to help you take the fresh, unprocessed food you already enjoy and expand your options into dozens of easy, inexpensive, delicious meals.

Why eat more raw food? One reason is simplicity. When you prepare food without cooking, you spend less time in the kitchen—in fact, you don't even need to be in a kitchen! Whether you want a quick and tasty meal at home or a healthful bite at work or in a dorm room or hotel, raw is the ultimate fast food.

Another reason to eat more greens, vegetables, and fruits is that these foods will help you maintain optimal weight and health. My recipes eliminate culprits linked to weight gain and degenerative diseases, including "bad carbs" (such as white sugar and white flour) and "bad fats" (such as saturated fats and trans-fatty acids). Moreover, raw greens, vegetables, fruits, nuts, and seeds contain vitamins, minerals, phytonutrients, enzymes, and fiber—all essential for good health. Better nutrition not only helps prevent disease and weight gain but also slows the aging process and increases energy.

Any diet you follow can be improved by eating more green leafy vegetables and less sugar and refined food. If you are a vegetarian or vegan, adding raw-food dishes to your repertoire will give you more nutrition and variety than cooked vegetables and starches alone. Only a small percentage of people follow a strict, all-raw diet all the time, but everyone can improve the meals they already enjoy by adding more raw food.

The simplest raw food needs no preparation whatsoever—just bite into an apple. At the other extreme are elaborate raw dishes that require expensive equipment, exotic ingredients, and considerable advance work (such as sprouting, fermenting, and dehydrating). My book aims at a happy medium between these extremes. The recipes call for only a few pieces of equipment, some of which you may already own, and all of which you can purchase conveniently and inexpensively. The ingredients featured are available at most grocery stores. Preparation techniques are simple, so that a kitchen novice can do fine.

There are many classic, delicious raw-food recipes available in books, magazines, and online, but only some are both tasty *and* easy. I've chosen recipes for this book that can be made in minutes, succeed every time, taste delicious, and can be eaten every day.

The book is organized into sections on breakfast, snacks, lunch, dinner, and dessert to take the guesswork out of what to eat when. Just turn to the menus (pages 62

1

to 64) or the introductory material in each section for guidelines. Eating entirely raw meals will leave you feeling satisfied, yet light. But if you want to add cooked food to a meal, it's easy to do, and each chapter provides suggestions. Moreover, when you're traveling, you don't need to leave healthful food behind. A new chapter, Raw On the Go (pages 154 to 156), will show you how to eat well on the road.

When considering a particular recipe, first note if advance preparation is required, such as soaking nuts. Most of the recipes can be made immediately if you keep a few basics on hand (see Advance Preparation, page 14). Once advance preparation is complete, get out the equipment and tools that you'll need, then prepare the ingredients as indicated. With everything ready, you will be able to put your meal together in minutes. If any ingredient, piece of equipment, or technique is unfamiliar to you, refer to the Glossary (page 194) or Tools and Techniques (page 9).

Two last points. First, the recipes in this book aim to please the average palate, so they call for moderate amounts of pungent seasonings, such as garlic, onion, cayenne, and salt. If you like your food highly seasoned, add more of these ingredients; if you don't, begin with small amounts, taste, and adjust. Second, recipes for one person are easily doubled to make food for two or leftovers. Recipes for two should not be halved, however, because the specified ingredient amounts allow a blender or food processor to work more efficiently. Just save any leftovers for the next day.

KITCHEN SETUP

Stocking your kitchen with the appropriate equipment and ingredients will make food preparation easy. The following is a comprehensive list of what you'll need. With these items on hand you can make any recipe in this book. But don't feel you need to buy everything at once. You can get started right away on many of the recipes—with just a knife, a cutting board, and a few staples.

Kitchen Equipment

To increase your efficiency, store equipment where you'll use it. Keep the juicer on the counter by the sink, for example, and put the blender and food processor on the counter where you chop. All other tools should be within easy reach of this counter.

BOWLS, PANS, AND UTENSILS

baking dish, glass (8-inch square)

bamboo sushi mat

bowls, small and medium

citrus juicer or reamer

colander

garlic press

grater, box

grater, file (Microplane brand; optional)

mandoline (optional)

Mason jars, widemouthed (pint-sized and quart-sized)

measuring cups, dry (various sizes)

measuring cups, liquid (1-cup and 2-cup sizes)

measuring spoons

mesh bag (for straining nut milks; optional)

peeler

pie plate, glass (9-inch)

ramekins, two (6-ounce; optional)

salad spinner

saucepan, small (for warming soups; optional)

spatula, rubber

spatula or pie server

strainer, fine-mesh

tart pan with removable bottom (9-inch)

tart pans, two, with removable bottoms (5-inch; optional)

tea kettle (optional)

tongs

vegetable spiral slicer (optional)

whisk

wooden spoon

ELECTRIC APPLIANCES

blender

coffee grinder (for grinding seeds)

food processor

ice-cream maker (optional)

juicer

KNIVES AND CUTTING BOARD

cutting board, wood or bamboo

honing steel

knife block or holder

knife, chef's (8-inch)

knife, paring

knife, serrated (5-inch)

knife sharpener (optional)

shears, kitchen

Staple Ingredients

Stock your kitchen with the following items and replenish them as needed. Store sesame oil in the refrigerator and extra-virgin olive oil at room temperature. Keep spices and dried fruits in a cool, dark cabinet, away from direct heat and light. Dates can be stored at room temperature for up to two months, in the refrigerator for six months, or in the freezer for one year. Make sure you purchase raw, not roasted, nuts and seeds. Store these in sealed containers in the refrigerator for up to three months or in the freezer for one year.

DRIED FRUITS

apples

dates, medjool

figs, black Mission

mangoes

prunes

raisins, dark

raisins, golden

FROZEN FRUITS

blackberries

blueberries

cherries

mangoes (optional)

peaches

raspberries

OILS AND VINEGARS

balsamic vinegar

cider vinegar

olive oil, extra-virgin

sesame oil, cold-pressed (optional)

DRIED HERBS AND SPICES

basil

black pepper, ground

cayenne

cinnamon, ground

cumin, ground

curry powder

dill weed

garlic powder

onion powder

oregano

paprika

RAW NUTS AND SEEDS

almonds

cashews

chia seeds

coconut, unsweetened shredded dried

flaxseeds, dark or golden

hempseeds (optional)

macadamia nuts (optional)

pecans

pine nuts (optional)

pumpkin seeds (optional)

sunflower seeds

walnuts

SWEETENERS

maple syrup or agave nectar

stevia, liquid (optional)

MISCELLANEOUS

almond butter, raw

almond extract

apple juice (optional)

arame

capers

carob powder

cocoa powder, unsweetened

dulse leaves or flakes (optional)

miso, mellow white

mustard, Dijon

nori sheets

oat groats, whole

oats, old-fashioned rolled

olives, kalamata, pitted

salt, unrefined

tahini, raw

tamari

tomatoes, sun-dried (dry or oil-packed)

vanilla extract

Weekly Groceries

When you have the following fresh ingredients on hand, you will be able to make most of the recipes in this book. The quantities listed are for one person; double them for two.

PRODUCE

apples, 4

avocados, 2

bananas, 4

basil, 1 bunch (about 2 ounces)

bell pepper, red, 1

cabbage, red or green, 1 head

carrots, 2

celery, 1 bunch

cilantro, 1 bunch (about 2 ounces)

cucumbers, 2

fruit, in season, 4 pieces

garlic, 1 head

kale or collard greens, 1 bunch (about 1 pound)

lemons, 2

lettuce (mesclun, one 5-ounce package; red leaf, 1 head; romaine, 1 head)

limes, 2

onion, 1

parsley, 1 bunch (about 2 ounces)

spinach, 1 bunch (10 to 16 ounces), or 1 (5-ounce) package baby spinach

Swiss chard, 1 bunch

tomatoes, 2

zucchini, 2

RAW BASICS

Soaking Raw Nuts and Seeds

Some recipes call for unsoaked nuts and seeds because a dry texture is preferred. When soaking is required for nondairy milks, sauces, salad dressings, and pâtés, put nuts or seeds in a Mason jar, fill with cool water, screw on the lid, and leave for the specified time (see table below) at room temperature. After soaking, always drain the nuts and seeds and let them air-dry in a colander or strainer for ten minutes before storing. This step will help retain their crunchy texture and preserve them longer. Stored in a sealed container in the refrigerator, soaked nuts will keep for five days and soaked sesame and sunflower seeds will keep for three days. After that they may turn a darker brown and taste a little bitter.

If a recipe calls for soaked nuts or seeds, measure them *after* soaking.

SOAKING TIMES FOR RAW NUTS AND SEEDS

NUTS OR SEEDS (1 CUP DRY)	SOAKING TIME	YIELD (SOAKED)
Almonds	8–12 hours	1½ cups
Brazil nuts	2 hours	1 cup
Cashews	2 hours	1 cup
Pecans	4–6 hours	1¼ cups
Sesame seeds	4–6 hours	1¼ cups
Sunflower seeds	6–8 hours	1⅓ cups
Walnuts	4–6 hours	1¼ cups

Soaking Dried Fruits

Each recipe that includes dried fruit specifies whether the fruit should be soaked or unsoaked. Dates, raisins, figs, and apricots should be soaked for ten to thirty minutes when creating recipes that call for a smooth consistency, such as nut and seed milks, sauces, puddings, and creamy pie fillings. When raisins, dried cherries, or dried cranberries are to be used in a salad, they will also benefit from soaking for a few minutes, to plump them up.

To soak dried fruit, put it in a bowl with enough water to cover and let soak for ten to thirty minutes. Drain well and use immediately.

Dried fruit that will be used in cakes, cookies, and pie crusts should not be soaked, or these desserts will turn out soggy. Sun-dried tomatoes, if purchased dry, should always be soaked for at least thirty minutes or up to two hours. Oil-packed sun-dried tomatoes need no soaking.

Storing and Ripening Produce

Most fruits, vegetables, and greens can be stored in the refrigerator. Bananas and to-matoes, however, should never be refrigerated, since they will turn mushy and lose flavor. Keep onions and garlic at room temperature. Some fruits, such as avocados, ba-nanas, pears, plums, peaches, and melons, will continue to ripen after they have been purchased. If they are not ripe initially, store them at room temperature until they are ready. Ripe avocados, plums, and peaches give slightly when you touch them. An un-ripe melon is rock hard near the round indentation at the stem end; in ripe melons, this area will be a little softer. Ripe bananas are yellow with brown freckles. Once avocados, pears, plums, peaches, and melons are nearly ripe, move them to the refrigerator if you are not going to eat them right away. They will usually keep for several more days.

If you need to store produce that has already been cut or torn, put it in a ziplock bag, press out as much air as possible, and store in the refrigerator. Torn greens and apple, avocado, and tomato halves will keep for two days. (Leave the pit in the avo-cado half that you are storing so it will retain more of its green color.) Cucumber and red bell pepper halves will keep for five days and onion halves for one week.

Cleaning Produce

Most fruits and vegetables can be cleaned with purified water. Produce with a thick skin that will not be peeled requires a vegetable brush for deeper cleaning. Mush-rooms should not be washed or they will become soggy. Wipe them with a lightly dampened paper towel.

Warming Up Raw Food

Most raw food tastes best at room temperature. Unless a dish is to be served chilled, remove it from the refriger-ator ten to thirty minutes before eating. To warm soup, pour it into a small saucepan and warm over low heat for two to three minutes, taking care not to overheat it.

To warm a dessert, preheat the oven to the lowest pos-sible temperature (no higher than 200 degrees F). Turn off the oven, insert the dessert, and warm for fifteen minutes. Alternatively, heat the dessert for thirty minutes in a food dehydrator set at 105 degrees F.

Greens require special care since they usually need to be dried after they are washed. If a recipe calls for whole leaves, clean them with a damp paper towel. This will eliminate the need for drying. To remove the stems from kale or collard greens, hold each leaf upside down by the end of the stem. Grip the sides of the protruding stem with the thumb and forefinger of your free hand. Draw your thumb and forefinger down the length of the stem, stripping off the leaf. For basil and spinach, simply pluck off the leaves with your fingers.

If a recipe calls for torn lettuce, tear the leaves before washing, then dry them in a salad spinner. You can also wash and dry whole basil and spinach leaves in the spinner. For fresh cilantro, dill, and parsley, hold the bunch by the stems and swish it around in a bowl of water. Shake well to dry, then press the bunch of herbs between layers of paper towels to remove any remaining moisture.

TOOLS AND TECHNIQUES

Your most important tools are good-quality knives and a sturdy cutting board. A few other pieces of manual equipment and some electric appliances make raw-food prep more varied, efficient, and fun.

Cutting Boards and Knives

Wood or bamboo cutting boards are preferable to plastic, which can chip and leach into food. Wood also has a bit of give, which makes chopping easier; plastic is so hard that it can dull knives. I recommend a large, sturdy board that won't slip. You can also buy a second lightweight board for small tasks. Use one side for fruit and the other for vegetables to avoid mixing flavors. Clean cutting boards with a damp sponge and mild dish soap.

An eight-inch chef's knife is essential for slicing, chopping, and mincing harder fruits and vegetables. A good one will last for years. To decide between a European-style chef's knife or an Asian-style santoku knife, hold each knife to see how it feels.

Learning to use these knives correctly will save you time and energy. Grip the handle close to where it joins the blade; put your thumb against the side or on top of the blade. Place the knife tip on the cutting board beyond the far side of the fruit or vegetable. Push gently down and forward, cutting with the middle portion of the blade. Pull back and repeat. Use your free hand to hold the fruit or vegetable, with your fingertips safely tucked under your knuckles.

A five-inch serrated knife or a paring knife is easiest for slicing softer fruits and vegetables (such as citrus fruits, kiwifruit, peaches, plums, tomatoes, mushrooms, and olives) and California Rolls (page 134). Unlike a chef's knife, these knives work best if you pull the blade toward you as you slice. A five-inch serrated knife is also useful for peeling citrus fruits when you don't want any of the white pith to appear. Cut off each end of the citrus fruit and put the top or bottom of the fruit flat on a cutting board. Following the curve of the fruit, cut away the peel on all sides. You can then use the knife to remove segments of the fruit by cutting them out from between the white membranes.

Knives require care. Always store them in a block or holder to protect them. To keep chef's and paring knives sharp, use a honing steel regularly (never use a steel on serrated knives). If the blades get dull, I recommend the Chef's Choice brand multi-edge manual sharpener; it is much easier to use than a traditional whetstone, and it works on both regular and serrated blades. In addition, I recommend having knives sharpened professionally once a year.

Learning basic knife techniques can both improve the appearance of your dishes and make kitchen work more efficient and enjoyable. Learning these skills from books alone can be difficult. See Resources (page 214) for recommended classes and videos, or enroll in a knife skills class at a cooking store or school. Most importantly, practice. Concentrate on accuracy, and speed will come.

Mincing Onions, Garlic, and Herbs

When mincing onions, garlic, or fresh herbs, use the "fan technique." Gather the chopped ingredients in a pile on the cutting board. Place the tip of a chef's knife or santoku knife on the far side of the pile. Rest your free hand on top of the blade. Keeping the knife tip on the board, move the blade up and down quickly as you pivot the base of the knife in a fan motion. Stop periodically to regather the pile of ingredients, and continue mincing until the desired texture is achieved. (Never scrape the sharp edge of the knife against the cutting board to push the ingredients together; this will dull the blade.) Use the back of the knife for scraping. Alternatively, mince ingredients in a food processor fitted with the S blade. Chop onions or herbs coarsely and peel garlic (leaving the cloves whole) before putting them in the processor. Pulse until the desired texture is achieved.

Here are tips for cutting fruits that require special attention.

- To peel an avocado, put it lengthwise on a cutting board. Cut in with a chef's knife until you hit the pit, then turn the avocado over while rotating the knife all the way around the pit. Twist the avocado to separate the halves. Push the lower part of the blade into the pit and twist the knife to pull out the pit. Scoop the flesh out of the peel with a spoon, then slice or mash.

- To thinly slice an apple or pear, cut off each end of the fruit and then peel it. Set the fruit on end on a cutting board and cut it in half lengthwise. Using a teaspoon, scoop out the core and seeds. Put each apple or pear half lengthwise on the board, cut-side down, and slice thinly.

- To peel and chop a mango, slice it lengthwise into quarters, cutting all around the pit. Scoop the flesh away from the peel with a spoon, discard the peel, and slice or chop the flesh. Alternatively, peel the mango with a paring knife, then slice or chop the flesh.

- To halve and slice a peach or nectarine, insert the blade of a chef's knife into the natural groove of the fruit. Press down until you reach the pit. Rotate the fruit vertically all the way around, continuing to press down on the pit. Twist the fruit to separate the halves. Push the lower part of the blade hard into the pit and twist the knife to pull out the pit. Put each half lengthwise on a cutting board, cut-side down, and slice thinly.

Other Manual Tools

A grater is useful for producing small amounts of shredded carrot or beet; for larger amounts, use a food processor fitted with a shredding disk. A file grater (Microplane brand) is wonderful for grating fresh ginger and nutmeg and for removing the zest from lemons, limes, and oranges.

Besides peeling, a vegetable peeler can make carrot "ribbons" to replace the shredded carrot in a Garden Wrap (page 133), a Spring Roll (page 137), or California Rolls (page 134). To make ribbons, use the peeler to produce long strips, rotating the carrot until there is nothing left to peel. You can make ribbons out of cucumbers and zucchini the same way, peeling them on all sides until you reach the core.

A vegetable spiral slicer, sometimes called a "spiralizer" or a garnishing machine, transforms zucchini, butternut squash, carrots, cucumbers, beets, parsnips, daikon radish, and celery root into delicate angel-hair "pasta." If you don't have a spiralizer, you can make zucchini "fettuccine" by creating zucchini ribbons with a vegetable peeler.

A mandoline is a great tool for cutting vegetables into ultrathin, uniform slices. It works especially well for cabbage, cucumbers, onions, carrots, beets, and fennel.

Many recipes require that tomatoes and cucumbers be seeded to improve the texture of the finished dish. To seed a tomato, first remove the nub at the stem end with a paring knife. Cut the tomato in half lengthwise. Scoop out the seeds with your thumb and fingers or with a spoon. To seed a cucumber, cut it in half lengthwise and scoop out the seeds with a spoon.

There's no need to spend $100 or more on a stainless steel French model; the inexpensive plastic versions work fine. You can also use a ceramic slicer (Kyocera brand) or a V slicer (Borner brand).

A mesh bag, also called a sprout bag or a nut milk bag, is useful for straining almond milk and other nut and seed milks. If you don't have a mesh bag, use a fine-mesh strainer.

A bamboo sushi mat is essential for making tight, professional-quality nori rolls. They are usually available in natural food stores and Asian markets for a dollar or two.

Electric Appliances

A blender is the right appliance for making smoothies and creamy soups, sauces, and salad dressings. An inexpensive model is all you need for the recipes in this book, though eventually you may want a high-speed blender, such as a Vitamix. When blending, begin with the softest ingredients and some of the liquid. Add the other ingredients and blend until the mixture is smooth, stopping occasionally to scrape down the blender jar with a rubber spatula. Pour in more of the liquid and process until the desired consistency is achieved.

A food processor chops, minces, grinds, and makes textured purées. With it you can produce delicious pâtés, chunky sauces, cakes, cookies, and pie crusts. An inexpensive model is fine to start with, but I recommend the Cuisinart brand for maximum performance and durability. A seven-cup food processor is ideal for making portions for one or two people and will work well for all the recipes in this book. To prepare food for large numbers of people, however, a fourteen-cup machine is essential. All food processors work best if they are filled no more than halfway with ingredients.

Food processors come with an S blade for chopping, grinding, mincing, and puréeing. When mincing, use the pulse button so you don't overprocess the ingredients. For all tasks involving the S blade, you may need to stop and scrape down the work bowl with a rubber spatula a few times. Most food processors also come with a slicing disk and a coarse shredding disk. The slicer is useful for large quantities of produce, and the shredder grates carrots and beets if you don't want to do it by hand. For extra-fine work, order a two-millimeter slicing disk and a "fine" shredding disk from Cuisinart to fit your particular model.

There are many types and brands of juicers on the market. They start at about $40, and if you are new to juicing, a basic model is fine. If you use the machine each morning, however, you may want to invest in a slow-speed model designed to extract the maximum juice from greens (see Glossary, page 195, for recommended brands). Slow-speed models also run at low temperatures, which preserves nutrients and enzymes. Juices made in one of these machines can be prepared several hours in advance, without significant loss of nutrients or taste.

Following Recipes and Measuring Ingredients

The ingredients in each recipe are listed in their order of use. Water is often added last to allow you to thin a recipe to the desired consistency. Avocados and fresh herbs are also often saved for last, since their delicate texture and taste can be adversely affected by overblending.

Before you measure, note how each ingredient is prepped. Is it chopped, ground, minced, shredded, sliced, or soaked? Are leaves firmly packed? Are dates pitted? Always prep the ingredients as specified before measuring them. For example, if a recipe calls for "1½ cups dates, soaked," measure the dates and then soak them. But if the recipe calls for "1½ cups soaked almonds," measure the almonds after soaking.

Purchase stainless steel dry measuring cups and spoons for maximum durability. Make sure you always fill the cup or spoon level even with the edge. Purchase liquid (glass or plastic) measuring cups in addition to dry measuring cups, because pouring from them is easier.

ADVANCE PREPARATION

Preparing some ingredients in advance each week takes about an hour and allows you to make most of the recipes in this book quickly.

Prepping Produce

As soon as you return from the grocery store, wash and dry all the vegetables. Tear lettuce into bite-sized pieces and store in a salad spinner in the refrigerator for up to three days. Most other vegetables can be sliced or shredded and stored in sealed glass jars or containers in the refrigerator for three to five days. For example, slice half a head of cabbage for salads and slaws, shred beets and carrots for Rainbow Salad (page 96), or separate broccoli into florets and slice carrots for Crudités (page 91). Avocados, cucumbers, fresh fruits, and tomatoes should be sliced just before using.

Making Seasonings

Many dishes call for small amounts of crushed garlic, minced onion, and lemon or lime juice. Since these items will keep for five days when stored in a sealed container in the refrigerator, you can save time by preparing larger quantities.

To crush garlic, separate the cloves with a chef's knife. To begin peeling, turn the knife on its side, rest your free hand on the blade, and press down on a few cloves at a time. This will loosen the peels. Peel each clove with your fingers. (To save time, prepeeled garlic cloves are available in the refrigerated produce section of many grocery stores.) Crush each clove separately in a garlic press or mince all of the cloves at once in a food processor, stopping occasionally to scrape down the work bowl with a rubber spatula.

To mince an onion, chop it into one-inch pieces. Put the onion in a food processor fitted with the S blade and pulse until minced. Do not overprocess or the onion may get watery. Alternatively, mince the onion by hand.

To make ½ cup of freshly squeezed lemon juice, cut four lemons in half crosswise. Extract the juice with a citrus juicer or reamer. For ½ cup of freshly squeezed lime juice, use eight limes. Stored in a sealed container, lemon or lime juice will keep in the refrigerator for five days or in the freezer for one month.

Minced fresh parsley or cilantro will keep in the refrigerator for three days. To mince parsley, hold the bunch firmly by the stem end and chop the leaves. Discard the stems or save them for Basic Green Juice (page 23). Continue to chop the leaves until they are minced. Alternatively, put the leaves in a food processor fitted with the S blade and pulse until minced.

Soaking and Grinding Nuts and Seeds

Soaked and drained nuts will keep in the refrigerator for five days and seeds will keep for three days, so you'll need to prepare them once or twice a week. Almond Milk (page 58) is a tasty alternative to dairy milk that you can drink straight, pour on cereal, or use as a base for shakes. Prepare Almond Milk using freshly soaked almonds.

Use a small, inexpensive coffee grinder to grind flaxseeds, which can be added to juices and smoothies. If you want to make cookies (see pages 163 and 164) during the week, prepare Almond Flour (page 165) in advance. For Multiseed Porridge (page 54), prepare Ground Seed Mix (page 57). Grinding nuts past the flour stage into a paste produces nut butter, which keeps for months in the refrigerator. Almond Butter and Cashew Butter (page 78) make delicious snacks with apple slices or celery sticks. Stored in a sealed container in the refrigerator, ground nuts and seeds will keep for three months.

Growing Sprouts

Some of the recipes in this book call for alfalfa or clover sprouts. You can purchase them in most grocery stores, but it is more economical to grow your own. Sprouting takes five days but only five minutes of your time per day. Draining the sprouts requires cheesecloth or mesh screening (the plastic kind used for windows). The screening is more durable than cheesecloth and can be purchased at your local hardware store. You can cut it into squares with kitchen shears.

To grow sprouts, put ¼ cup of alfalfa or clover seeds in a quart-sized Mason jar. Fill with water and screw on the band with its lid. Let soak for 8 to 12 hours. Remove the band and lid and put a square of cheesecloth or mesh screening on top

Freezing Bananas for Smoothies and Shakes

Once bananas get too ripe to eat, freeze them to use in smoothies and shakes. Put the bananas on a plate and set in the freezer for one hour. (This will prevent them from sticking together.) Transfer to a ziplock bag and press out as much air as possible before sealing the bag and returning the bananas to the freezer. Frozen bananas will keep for one month.

of the jar. Screw on the band over the cheesecloth or mesh. To rinse and drain the seeds, pour out the soaking water, add fresh water through the cheesecloth or mesh, and pour it out.

Invert the jar on a dish rack so the seeds continue to drain. Let the sprouts grow this way for five days, rinsing and draining them each morning and evening. On the last day, put the jar by a window for 4 to 6 hours; the sunlight will turn the sprouts green.

Remove the sprouts from the jar and put them in a medium bowl filled with water. Swish them around to loosen their hulls. Holding the sprouts down with one hand, tip the bowl into the sink to drain off the hulls and the water. Put the sprouts in a colander to air-dry for thirty minutes. Stored in a sealed container or jar in the refrigerator, green leafy sprouts will keep for five days.

Make-Ahead Recipes

If you want to do more advance preparation, many dips, pâtés, sauces, salad dressings, and desserts will keep for several days. If you make two salad dressings and two pâtés, you will have enough for the week. Juices, smoothies, soups, and salads are best prepared fresh, but if you are in a rush in the morning, chop the vegetables the night before.

Many recipes in this book can be used in a variety of ways, so preparing a larger batch in advance doesn't mean you have to eat the same thing every day. For example, Not Tuna Pâté (page 71) can be included in a salad, Stuffed Bell Pepper (page 142), Not Tuna Sandwich (page 125), or Not Tuna Roll (page 134). Walnut Pâté (page 72) can be used in a Walnut Pâté Sandwich (page 127), Not Meatballs (page 136), or a Tomato Stack (page 140). Chocolate Mousse (page 180) can be eaten straight, layered with Vanilla Crème Sauce (page 185) in a parfait, or used to fill a Chocolate Pie or Tart with Strawberries (page 177). As you become familiar with the recipes, you'll discover your own favorites to make in advance.

breakfast

To start the day with energy, keep your morning meal light. Juices, green smoothies, and fresh fruits are perfect, since they are high in nutrients yet low in calories and easy to digest. If you need something heartier in the morning, try a raw cereal, such as Granola (page 53) or Multiseed Porridge (page 54) with Almond Milk (page 58).

JUICES

An easy way for busy people to get needed vegetables is drinking juice—as a cleansing, nutritious breakfast or an energizing midafternoon snack. Use organically grown produce whenever possible, especially when juicing greens. Basic Green Juice (page 23) and Energizing-Purifying Juice (page 21) should be your staples, since they are the highest in nutrients and lowest in calories and sugars. The other juices in this section will provide variety during the week. If you are sensitive to sugars, limit your consumption of beet, carrot, and fruit juices. Instead, choose juices made from green leafy vegetables.

Juicing is a great opportunity to use vegetable scraps left over from other recipes. Save broccoli stalks, parsley stems, and other odds and ends and juice them with a base of carrots, celery, or cucumbers. For easier digestion and better absorption of nutrients, drink juices on an empty stomach. A high-quality machine extracts more juice from the produce and preserves more nutrients. (For information on juicers, see Tools and Techniques, page 13.)

When you juice, cut the fruits and vegetables into chunks that will fit comfortably through the machine's chute. If you are using a slow-speed juicer designed for greens, do not remove the stems from cilantro, collard greens, kale, and parsley or cut the greens into pieces. Simply feed them stem first into the machine. Start and finish the juicing process with carrots or celery, since they are firm and easy to juice. Don't leave garlic and ginger until the end—juicing other vegetables afterward helps push any remaining pieces of garlic and ginger through the machine.

Use Granny Smith apples for a tart, less sweet juice.

pink apple juice

YIELD: 1 CUP, 1 SERVING

2 apples, unpeeled and cut into chunks

1 beet, scrubbed and cut into chunks

1 lime, peeled

1 (¼-inch) piece fresh ginger

EQUIPMENT

cutting board

chef's knife, 8-inch

serrated knife, 5-inch

juicer

Juice all of the ingredients, and serve immediately.

Per serving: calories: 204, protein: 2 g, fat: 1 g, carbohydrate: 43 g, fiber: 10 g, sodium: 61 mg
Note: The nutritional values for this recipe are based on the whole-food ingredients, before juicing.

Carrot juice blends are excellent sources of beta-carotene.

carrot-celery-beet juice

YIELD: 2 CUPS, 1 SERVING

4 stalks celery

2 apples, unpeeled and cut into chunks (optional)

1 large carrot, scrubbed

1 beet, scrubbed and cut into chunks

1 lime, peeled (optional)

EQUIPMENT

cutting board

chef's knife, 8-inch

juicer

Juice all of the ingredients, and serve immediately.

Per serving: calories: 96, protein: 3 g, fat: 1 g, carbohydrate: 15 g, fiber: 6 g, sodium: 215 mg
Note: The nutritional values for this recipe are based on the whole-food ingredients, before juicing.

Start the morning hydrated and refreshed with this easy juice.

carrot-celery-cucumber juice

YIELD: 2 CUPS, 1 SERVING

4 stalks celery

2 carrots, scrubbed

1 cucumber, unpeeled and
sliced lengthwise

EQUIPMENT

cutting board

chef's knife, 8-inch

juicer

Juice all of the ingredients, and serve immediately.

Per serving: calories: 130, protein: 4 g, fat: 1 g, carbohydrate: 21 g, fiber: 8 g, sodium: 233 mg
Note: The nutritional values for this recipe are based on the whole-food ingredients, before juicing.

Carrots and apples are a wonderfully sweet combination. I love the ginger kick at
the end of each sip.

carrot-apple-ginger juice

YIELD: 2 CUPS, 1 SERVING

3 carrots, scrubbed

2 apples, unpeeled and cut
into chunks

1 (1-inch) **piece of fresh
ginger**

EQUIPMENT

cutting board

chef's knife, 8-inch

juicer

Juice all of the ingredients, and serve immediately.

Per serving: calories: 251, protein: 3 g, fat: 2 g, carbohydrate: 50 g, fiber: 14 g, sodium: 167 mg
Note: The nutritional values for this recipe are based on the whole-food ingredients, before juicing.

This juice detoxifies the body while providing needed nutrients and energy. It is a health-promoting daily breakfast and a revitalizing snack. To save time, wash and cut the vegetables the night before. For a spicier juice, add the optional ginger and radish.

energizing-purifying juice

YIELD: 1½ CUPS, 1 SERVING

2 stalks celery

1 carrot, scrubbed

⅛ head green or red cabbage, cut into chunks

¼ cucumber, unpeeled and sliced lengthwise

4 leaves kale or collard greens

10 sprigs parsley

¼ cup coarsely chopped broccoli stalks

1 small red radish, or 1 (1-inch) piece daikon radish (optional)

1 (¼-inch) piece fresh ginger (optional)

1½ teaspoons freshly squeezed lemon juice
(¼ lemon; optional)

EQUIPMENT

cutting board

chef's knife, 8-inch

measuring cups

juicer

citrus juicer or reamer

measuring spoons

spoon

Juice the celery, carrot, cabbage, cucumber, kale, parsley, broccoli, and optional radish and ginger. Stir in the lemon juice if desired. Alternatively, peel the lemon and put it through the juicer with the vegetables. Serve immediately.

SOOTHING ALOE JUICE: Stir 1 tablespoon of aloe vera juice into the finished juice. Aloe vera provides amino acids and soothes the digestive tract.

SWEET ENERGIZING-PURIFYING JUICE: Add ¼ unpeeled Granny Smith apple or ¼ scrubbed beet or both. If using the beet, 2 to 3 leaves of beet greens may be added. People who aren't used to the taste of vegetable juice often prefer this sweeter variation.

Per serving: calories: 126, protein: 6 g, fat: 1 g, carbohydrate: 18 g, fiber: 9 g, sodium: 178 mg
Note: The nutritional values for this recipe are based on the whole-food ingredients, before juicing.

This juice contains the same detoxifying ingredients as Energizing-Purifying Juice (page 21) but in larger quantities to provide a full day's supply. Diluting juice with water makes it appropriate for a fast. Include the apple or beet (or both) if you prefer a sweeter taste.

fasting juice

YIELD: 6 CUPS, 1 FULL DAY'S SUPPLY

½ head green or red cabbage, cut into chunks

16 leaves (about 1 bunch) kale or collard greens

8 stalks celery

4 carrots, scrubbed

1 cucumber, unpeeled and sliced lengthwise

1 Granny Smith apple, unpeeled and cut into chunks (optional)

1 beet, scrubbed (with the beet greens, if available; optional)

1 cup coarsely chopped broccoli stalks

2 ounces (about 1 bunch) parsley

4 small red radishes, or 1 (4-inch) piece daikon (optional)

1 (1-inch) piece fresh ginger (optional)

2 tablespoons freshly squeezed lemon juice (1 lemon; optional)

3 cups purified water

EQUIPMENT

cutting board

chef's knife, 8-inch

measuring cups

juicer

citrus juicer or reamer

measuring spoons

spoon

fine-mesh strainer

Juice the cabbage, kale, celery, carrots, cucumber, optional apple, optional beet, broccoli, parsley, radishes, and ginger. Stir in the lemon juice if desired. Alternatively, peel the lemon and put it through the juicer with the vegetables. Strain the juice through a fine-mesh strainer. Dilute the juice with the water if desired. Store it in the refrigerator and drink throughout the day.

Per serving (6 cups): calories: 510, protein: 25 g, fat: 5 g, carbohydrate: 74 g, fiber: 35 g, sodium: 720 mg
Note: The nutritional values for this recipe are based on the whole-food ingredients, before juicing.

This nutritional powerhouse provides vitamins, calcium, and trace minerals. It is also low in calories and sugars, making it an ideal weight-loss drink. For a spicier green juice, include the optional ginger.

basic green juice

3 stalks celery

3 leaves kale or collard greens

½ cucumber, unpeeled and sliced lengthwise

10 sprigs parsley or cilantro, or some of each (optional)

1 (¼-inch) piece fresh ginger (optional)

1½ teaspoons freshly squeezed lemon juice (¼ lemon)

EQUIPMENT

cutting board

chef's knife, 8-inch

juicer

citrus juicer or reamer

measuring spoons

spoon

Juice the celery, kale, cucumber, and optional parsley and ginger. Stir in the lemon juice. Alternatively, peel the lemon and put it through the juicer with the vegetables. Serve immediately.

SWEET GREEN JUICE: Add ½ Granny Smith apple, unpeeled and cut into chunks, or ½ cup of chopped pineapple. Alternatively, add 2 drops of liquid stevia to the finished juice.

Per serving: calories: 62, protein: 3 g, fat: 1 g, carbohydrate: 10 g, fiber: 4 g, sodium: 121 mg
Note: The nutritional values for this recipe are based on the whole-food ingredients, before juicing.

You can increase the antioxidant content of green juice by adding multiple greens and broccoli stalks. But don't worry about a bitter taste—the celery, cucumbers, and romaine lettuce keep this juice gentle.

super green juice

YIELD: 5 CUPS, 2 LARGE SERVINGS

1 head celery

1 head romaine lettuce, sliced lengthwise to fit your juicer

12 leaves (about 1 small bunch) **kale or collard greens**

4 cups spinach leaves, firmly packed

2 cucumbers, unpeeled and sliced lengthwise

2 Granny Smith apples, unpeeled and cut into chunks

1 cup coarsely chopped broccoli stalks

2 tablespoons freshly squeezed lemon juice (1 lemon)

EQUIPMENT

cutting board

chef's knife, 8-inch

measuring cups

juicer

citrus juicer or reamer

measuring spoons

spoon

Juice the celery, lettuce, kale, spinach, cucumbers, apples, and broccoli. Stir in the lemon juice. Alternatively, peel the lemon and put it through the juicer with the vegetables. Serve immediately, or store in the refrigerator to drink throughout the day.

Per serving: calories: 268, protein: 15 g, fat: 3 g, carbohydrate: 44 g, fiber: 15 g, sodium: 318 mg
Note: The nutritional values for this recipe are based on the whole-food ingredients, before juicing.

parfait of Strawberry Cashew Yogurt, *page 36,* **blueberries, strawberries, and Muesli,** *page 55*

Apple Sandwiches, *page 131,* **with Almond Butter,** *page 78*

Citrus juice from the store has been pasteurized, so vitamins and enzymes are lost. Freshly squeezed citrus juice takes just minutes to make, packs in a full day's supply of vitamin C, and tastes great.

citrus sunshine juice

YIELD: 1 CUP, 1 SERVING

2 oranges, cut in half crosswise

1 grapefruit, cut in half crosswise

½ lemon

EQUIPMENT

cutting board

chef's knife, 8-inch

citrus juicer or reamer

Extract the juice from all the fruit with a citrus juicer or reamer. Serve immediately.

Per serving: calories: 185, protein: 4 g, fat: 1 g, carbohydrate: 40 g, fiber: 8 g, sodium: 3 mg
Note: The nutritional values for this recipe are based on the whole-food ingredients, before juicing.

Popular at spas, this refreshing elixir makes eight glasses of water a pleasure to drink.

cucumber lemon water

YIELD: 8 CUPS, 1 DAY'S SUPPLY

8 cups purified water

½ cucumber, unpeeled and thinly sliced

½ lemon, unpeeled and thinly sliced

EQUIPMENT

measuring cups

cutting board

chef's knife, 8-inch

large pitcher or jar

Combine all the ingredients in a large pitcher or jar. Let sit for 8 to 12 hours at room temperature or in the refrigerator before serving. Drink throughout the day. Stored at room temperature or in the refrigerator, Cucumber Lemon Water will keep for 24 hours.

Per serving: calories: 0, protein: 0 g, fat: 0 g, carbohydrate: 0 g, fiber: 0 g, sodium: 0 mg

Taste this zippy homemade cocktail, and you'll never go back to juice in a can.

V-7 juice

YIELD: 1 CUP, 1 SERVING

2 stalks celery

1 tomato, quartered

½ red bell pepper, cut into chunks

⅛ cucumber, unpeeled and sliced lengthwise

10 sprigs parsley or cilantro

1 clove garlic

1½ teaspoons freshly squeezed lemon juice (¼ lemon)

Dash cayenne or hot sauce (optional)

EQUIPMENT

cutting board

chef's knife, 8-inch

juicer

citrus juicer or reamer

measuring spoons

spoon

Juice the celery, tomato, bell pepper, cucumber, parsley, and garlic. Stir in the lemon juice and cayenne if desired. Alternatively, peel the lemon and put it through the juicer with the vegetables. Serve immediately.

Per serving: calories: 66, protein: 3 g, fat: 1 g, carbohydrate: 9 g, fiber: 4 g, sodium: 84 mg
Note: The nutritional values for this recipe are based on the whole-food ingredients, before juicing.

FRUITS

Children are instinctively drawn to the bright colors, curved shapes, and sweet, juicy flavors of fruit. It is excellent for adults too, since it's easy to digest, high in vitamins, and a natural way to satisfy our love of sweets. Eat fruit first thing in the morning or a couple of hours after drinking fresh vegetable juice. If you are sensitive to sugars, limit yourself to small amounts.

When you're short on time, smoothies make a fast and energizing breakfast. If you like frosty smoothies, use frozen berries.

berry smoothie

YIELD: 1½ CUPS, 1 SERVING

1 banana

1 cup fresh or frozen strawberries, blueberries, or blackberries

¼ cup water

EQUIPMENT

measuring cups

blender

rubber spatula

Put all the ingredients in a blender and process on medium speed until smooth. Serve immediately.

GOJI BERRY SMOOTHIE: Soak ¼ cup of dried goji berries in the water for 30 minutes. Process the goji berries and their soaking water with the banana and strawberries.

GRAPE SMOOTHIE: Replace the berries with 1 cup of red seedless grapes and omit the water.

MANGO SMOOTHIE: Replace the berries with 1 cup of fresh or frozen mango chunks.

ORANGE AND BERRY SMOOTHIE: Add ½ orange, peeled, sectioned, and seeded.

PEACH SMOOTHIE: Replace the berries with 1 cup of fresh or frozen peach slices.

PROTEIN AND OMEGA-3 SMOOTHIE: Increase the water to 1 cup and add 2 tablespoons of raw vegan protein powder (see Glossary, page 201) and 1 tablespoon of ground flaxseeds.

QUICK GREEN SMOOTHIE: Add 1 tablespoon of green powder (see Glossary, page 199).

Per serving: calories: 149, protein: 2 g, fat: 1 g, carbohydrate: 32 g, fiber: 6 g, sodium: 3 mg

Pineapple flavor shines in this drink, which skips the rum and coconut.

piña colada smoothie

YIELD: 1½ CUPS, 1 SERVING

1 banana, fresh or frozen and thawed for 5 minutes, broken into 2 or 3 pieces

½ cup chopped fresh pineapple

½ orange, peeled, sectioned, and seeded

EQUIPMENT

measuring cups

blender

rubber spatula

Put all the ingredients in a blender and process on medium speed until smooth. Serve immediately.

Per serving: calories: 175, protein: 2 g, fat: 1 g, carbohydrate: 39 g, fiber: 6 g, sodium: 3 mg

A one-ingredient wonder to make melon lovers rejoice.

cantaloupe smoothie

YIELD: 1 CUP, 1 SERVING

½ small cantaloupe, seeded

EQUIPMENT

cutting board

chef's knife, 8-inch

spoon

blender

rubber spatula

Scoop out the cantaloupe flesh and put it in a blender. Process on medium speed until smooth. Serve immediately.

Per serving: calories: 91, protein: 2 g, fat: 1 g, carbohydrate: 19 g, fiber: 2 g, sodium: 43 mg

This simple breakfast tastes like a gourmet dessert. The berries turn the cream a lovely purplish pink.

berries and almond cream

YIELD: 1 SERVING

1 cup fresh blackberries, blueberries, raspberries, sliced strawberries, or a combination

1 teaspoon maple syrup or agave nectar

½ cup Almond Cream (page 58)

EQUIPMENT

measuring cups

measuring spoons

small bowl

rubber spatula

wine glass

Put the berries and maple syrup in a small bowl and toss gently to combine. Transfer to a wine glass and top with the Almond Cream. Serve immediately.

BERRIES AND CASHEW CREAM: Replace the Almond Cream with ½ cup of Cashew Cream (page 60).

Per serving: calories: 233, protein: 7 g, fat: 13 g, carbohydrate: 20 g, fiber: 11 g, sodium: 2 mg

This naturally sweet compote is delicious plain or with your favorite raw cereal (see pages 52 to 56).

dried fruit compote

YIELD: 1 SERVING

¼ cup water

4 pitted prunes or dried apricots

⅛ teaspoon lemon or orange zest (optional)

Dash ground cinnamon

EQUIPMENT

measuring cups

file grater (Microplane brand; optional)

measuring spoons

small bowl

fork

Put all the ingredients in a small bowl and stir to combine. Let soak for 8 to 12 hours at room temperature. Mash lightly with a fork. Stored in a sealed container in the refrigerator, Dried Fruit Compote will keep for 3 days.

Per serving: calories: 112, protein: 1 g, fat: 0 g, carbohydrate: 26 g, fiber: 3 g, sodium: 2 mg

Avocado makes a creamy, hearty contribution to this fruit salad. Enjoy it for breakfast or brunch.

avocado fruit salad

YIELD: 2 SERVINGS

1 avocado, diced

1 banana, diced

1 cup fresh raspberries, blueberries, or diced strawberries

EQUIPMENT

cutting board

chef's knife, 8-inch

measuring cups

small bowl

rubber spatula

Put all the ingredients in a small bowl and toss gently to combine. Serve immediately.

Per serving: calories: 227, protein: 3 g, fat: 14 g, carbohydrate: 16 g, fiber: 11 g, sodium: 8 mg

A rich array of red, pink, and purple makes this fruit platter as beautiful as it is tasty.

summer fruit platter

YIELD: 2 SERVINGS

1 small bunch red seedless grapes

2 plums

½ cup fresh cherries

½ cup fresh strawberries

4 fresh purple figs (optional)

2 small wedges watermelon (optional)

EQUIPMENT

measuring cups

serving platter or plate

Arrange the fruit attractively on a platter. Serve immediately.

Per serving: calories: 79, protein: 1 g, fat: 0 g, carbohydrate: 17 g, fiber: 3 g, sodium: 1 mg

Lazy mornings feel like vacation when you pair tropical fruits with lusciously scented Sweet Orange Cream Sauce (page 185).

tropical fruit salad

SEE PHOTO FACING PAGE 25.   **YIELD: 1 SERVING**

1 mango, or ½ small papaya, cubed

½ banana, sliced

1 kiwifruit, peeled and sliced

½ cup fresh raspberries or sliced strawberries

¼ cup **Sweet Orange Cream Sauce** (page 185; optional)

EQUIPMENT

cutting board

chef's knife, 8-inch

paring knife

measuring cups

small bowl

spoon

Put the mango, banana, kiwifruit, and berries in a small bowl and toss gently with a spoon. Serve immediately, with the Sweet Orange Cream Sauce if desired.

Per serving: calories: 264, protein: 3 g, fat: 2 g, carbohydrate: 55 g, fiber: 12 g, sodium: 8 mg

Homemade applesauce tastes better than the jarred variety—and it takes five minutes!

applesauce

YIELD: 1 CUP, 2 SERVINGS

2 apples, any variety, peeled, cored, and chopped

⅛ teaspoon ground cinnamon

¼ cup water, if needed to thin

EQUIPMENT

cutting board

peeler

chef's knife, 8-inch

measuring spoons

measuring cups

blender

rubber spatula

Put the apples and cinnamon in a blender and process on medium speed until smooth. Add the water, 2 tablespoons at a time, to achieve the desired consistency. Stored in a sealed container in the refrigerator, Applesauce will keep for 3 days.

Per serving: calories: 63, protein: 0 g, fat: 0 g, carbohydrate: 14 g, fiber: 2 g, sodium: 0 mg

When glazed with raspberry jam, fresh strawberries glisten and taste even sweeter.

strawberries with raspberry jam

YIELD: 4 SERVINGS

8 ounces frozen raspberries, thawed and drained (1 cup)

12 pitted medjool dates, soaked in water for 10 minutes and drained (see page 7)

2 cups fresh strawberries

EQUIPMENT

small colander or fine-mesh strainer

small bowl

blender

rubber spatula

measuring cups

Put the raspberries and dates in a blender and process on medium speed until smooth. Serve as a dip with the strawberries. Stored in a sealed container in the refrigerator, Raspberry Jam will keep for 5 days.

Per serving: calories: 120, protein: 1 g, fat: 1 g, carbohydrate: 24 g, fiber: 6 g, sodium: 1 mg

This simple pudding is fat-free, yet creamy and satisfying.

papaya-banana breakfast pudding

YIELD: 1 SERVING

1 small papaya, mashed (see note)

1 banana, thinly sliced

EQUIPMENT

cutting board

chef's knife, 8-inch

spoon

small bowl

fork

Put the papaya in a small bowl and top with the banana. Serve immediately.

NOTE: To mash the flesh of a papaya, first cut the fruit in half lengthwise. Scoop the seeds out with a spoon and discard them. Scoop the remaining flesh out of each half and put it in a small bowl. Mash with a fork.

Per serving: calories: 220, protein: 3 g, fat: 1 g, carbohydrate: 47 g, fiber: 8 g, sodium: 10 mg

Chia seeds thicken this fruity pudding to a pleasing tapioca-like texture.

chia-blueberry breakfast pudding

YIELD: 1½ CUPS, 2 SERVINGS

1½ cups fresh or thawed and drained frozen blueberries

½ orange, peeled, sectioned, and seeded

4 pitted medjool dates, soaked in water for 10 minutes and drained (see page 7)

2 tablespoons chia seeds, unsoaked

EQUIPMENT

measuring cups

small colander or fine-mesh strainer

cutting board

serrated knife, 5-inch

small bowl

measuring spoons

blender

rubber spatula

Put the blueberries, orange sections, and dates in a blender and process on medium speed until smooth. Add the chia seeds and process on high speed until well incorporated. Cover and refrigerate for at least 30 minutes before serving. Stored in a sealed container in the refrigerator, Chia-Blueberry Breakfast Pudding will keep for 24 hours.

Per serving: calories: 185, protein: 4 g, fat: 3 g, carbohydrate: 33 g, fiber: 5 g, sodium: 2 mg

Cashews, not dairy products, are the secret to this creamy delight. Serve plain, or with Muesli (page 55) and sliced strawberries.

strawberry cashew yogurt

SEE PHOTO FACING PAGE 24.

YIELD: 1 CUP, 2 SERVINGS

1½ cups fresh strawberries (about 12), hulled

½ cup soaked cashews (see page 7)

1 tablespoon maple syrup or agave nectar

1 teaspoon freshly squeezed lemon juice

Sliced fresh strawberries, for serving (optional)

EQUIPMENT

measuring cups

cutting board

paring knife

measuring spoons

citrus juicer or reamer

blender

rubber spatula

Put all the ingredients in a blender and process on medium speed until smooth. Serve with sliced strawberries if desired. Stored in a sealed container in the refrigerator, Strawberry Cashew Yogurt will keep for 3 days.

Per serving: calories: 272, protein: 8 g, fat: 17 g, carbohydrate: 24 g, fiber: 4 g, sodium: 6 mg

GREEN SMOOTHIES

Years ago, "smoothie" meant a sweet beverage made from fruit, fruit juice, ice, and sometimes sugar and milk. Health-conscious people might have also included soy milk, yogurt, or honey, or added protein powder or other supplements. But in the new millennium, smoothies have undergone a revolution. The "green smoothie," popularized by Victoria Boutenko in *Green for Life*, is a simpler and more healthful drink made by blending fresh fruits, leafy greens, and water. Not too bitter and not too sweet, green smoothies are fresh, creamy, and delicious. Kids love them, and so do people who typically shun green vegetables. Quick to make and consume, today's smoothies are the definition of ease and convenience.

If green smoothies were the only raw-food recipes in your repertoire, you'd be making a substantial contribution to your health. Greens are nutritional powerhouses, containing vitamins, minerals, phytonutrients, fiber, protein, and even small amounts of essential omega-3 fatty acids. Greens are the most important food you can eat, but most people don't get enough of them.

For many, the challenge is making greens palatable and digestible. Greens have tough cellulose fibers and need to be chewed thoroughly. Chewing huge salads can be time consuming and arduous for the beginner, and they are not always easy to digest. Here's where the blender comes in. It "chews" the greens for you, breaking down the cell walls and releasing the nutrients. So a green smoothie gives you all the goodness of greens without anything superfluous—no sugar or dairy products (as is often the case in conventional smoothies) and no salt or oil (as in many salads).

To make a green smoothie, start with a good blender. A high-speed model, such as a Vitamix, is ideal because it blends the greens, including tough stems, completely and allows you to make up to eight cups of smoothie. But a basic blender will work fine. You just need to remove tough stems, add a little more water, and work in batches if you're making a large amount.

Try Apple-Banana Green Smoothie (page 39) and Blueberry Green Smoothie (page 41) for inexpensive drinks made with readily available ingredients. Nonsweet Green Smoothie (page 40) and Garden Vegetable Green Smoothie (page 50) are perfect when you want a savory alternative. Other recipes in this chapter provide variety and feature seasonal ingredients.

You can improvise your own green smoothie by using your favorite ingredients. The basic formula for one (2-cup) serving is ⅔ cup of water, 2 cups of fruit, and 1 to 2 cups of greens.

Put the ⅔ cup of water in the blender first, to allow for easy blending. If you are using very watery fruits, such as grapes, mango, melon, or pineapple, you may not need as much water. Then add 2 cups of fresh or frozen fruit. (If you like, you can use the nonsweet "veg-etable" fruits, such as cucumbers, tomatoes, zucchini, or a combination.) Finally, add 1 to 2 cups of coarsely chopped greens (remove tough stems if necessary). The greens can be light (such as celery or romaine lettuce), medium (such as spinach or Swiss chard), or dark (such as kale, collard greens, or dandelion greens). You can even include fresh herbs (such as parsley, mint, or basil). If your palate isn't used to greens, use fewer of them, and be sure to include some of the lighter greens. Process all the ingredients on high speed until smooth, adding more water if needed.

For additional fiber and omega-3 fatty acids, include 1 tablespoon of ground flaxseeds or Ground Seed Mix (page 57). If you want more protein, add 1 tablespoon of raw vegan protein powder (see Glossary, page 201). You can also replace the water with a nut or seed milk, such as Almond Milk (page 58), Hemp Milk (page 57), or Coconut Milk (page 59).

Green smoothies make a great breakfast, or even a light lunch or dinner. You might wish to double the recipe. This way, you can sip a large smoothie throughout the morning. Store the rest in the refrigerator and have it as an appetizer with lunch or dinner or as a midafter-noon snack. Many green smoothies will keep for twenty-four hours.

Since apples and bananas are readily available, this smoothie is easy and affordable year round.

apple-banana green smoothie

1 cup water

2 apples, unpeeled and chopped

1 banana

2 cups chopped spinach or Swiss chard, packed

1 cup chopped kale or collard greens, packed

EQUIPMENT

measuring cups

cutting board

chef's knife, 8-inch

blender

rubber spatula

Put all the ingredients in a blender and process on high speed until smooth. Stored in a sealed jar in the refrigerator, Apple-Banana Green Smoothie will keep for 24 hours.

Per serving: calories: 138, protein: 4 g, fat: 1 g, carbohydrate: 28 g, fiber: 6 g, sodium: 61 mg

More savory than sweet, this smoothie is filled with nutrient-rich greens. It's one of my favorites for breakfast or a snack.

nonsweet green smoothie

YIELD: 2 CUPS, 1 SERVING

⅔ cup water

¼ cucumber, unpeeled and chopped

½ stalk celery, chopped

½ apple, unpeeled and chopped

½ cup chopped kale, packed

½ cup chopped romaine lettuce

¼ cup chopped fresh parsley, packed

⅛ lemon, peeled

EQUIPMENT

measuring cups

cutting board

chef's knife, 8-inch

blender

rubber spatula

Put all the ingredients in a blender and process on high speed until smooth. Stored in a sealed jar in the refrigerator, Nonsweet Green Smoothie will keep for 12 hours.

Per serving: calories: 78, protein: 3 g, fat: 1 g, carbohydrate: 13 g, fiber: 4 g, sodium: 43 mg

This smoothie is great for kids because the blueberries make it purple.

blueberry green smoothie

SEE PHOTO ON FRONT COVER.   YIELD: 2½ CUPS, 1 SERVING

½ cup water

1 orange, peeled, sectioned, and seeded

1 banana

1¼ cups (6 ounces) **frozen blueberries or mixed berries**

1½ cups chopped spinach, Swiss chard, or kale, packed

EQUIPMENT

measuring cups

cutting board

chef's knife, 8-inch

blender

rubber spatula

Put all the ingredients in a blender and process on high speed until smooth. Serve immediately.

Per serving: calories: 288, protein: 6 g, fat: 2 g, carbohydrate: 57 g, fiber: 13 g, sodium: 71 mg

In this kid-friendly (and kid-at-heart-friendly) smoothie, chocolate conceals the color and taste of spinach.

chocolate green smoothie

YIELD: 3 CUPS, 2 SERVINGS

1¼ cups water

2 bananas

4 pitted medjool dates, soaked in water for 10 minutes and drained

3½ tablespoons unsweetened cocoa powder

3 cups chopped spinach or Swiss chard, packed

EQUIPMENT

measuring cups

small bowl

small colander or fine-mesh strainer

measuring spoons

cutting board

chef's knife, 8-inch

blender

rubber spatula

Put all the ingredients in a blender and process on high speed until smooth. Serve immediately.

Per serving: calories: 188, protein: 6 g, fat: 2 g, carbohydrate: 37 g, fiber: 9 g, sodium: 70 mg

This smoothie is so sweet, you'll hardly believe it's loaded with dark leafy greens. Think of it as a green milkshake.

frosty banana-apple green smoothie

YIELD: 2½ CUPS, 2 SERVINGS

¾ cup water

2 frozen bananas (see page 15), thawed for 5 minutes and broken into 2 or 3 pieces

1 apple, unpeeled and chopped

8 leaves kale, chopped

EQUIPMENT

measuring cups

cutting board

chef's knife, 8-inch

blender

rubber spatula

Put all the ingredients in a blender and process on high speed until smooth. Serve immediately.

Per serving: calories: 164, protein: 4 g, fat: 1 g, carbohydrate: 35 g, fiber: 6 g, sodium: 30 mg

Too busy to make breakfast? This smoothie is quick.

simple berry green smoothie

YIELD: 2½ CUPS, 1 SERVING

¾ cup water

1½ cups fresh raspberries or blueberries

1 banana

2 cups chopped spinach or Swiss chard, packed

EQUIPMENT

measuring cups

cutting board

chef's knife

blender

rubber spatula

Put all the ingredients in a blender and process on high speed until smooth. Serve immediately.

Per serving: calories: 223, protein: 7 g, fat: 2 g, carbohydrate: 35 g, fiber: 17 g, sodium: 91 mg

Love the smell of succulent peaches? This smoothie will fill your kitchen with their aroma on summer mornings.

peachy apple green smoothie

YIELD: 2 CUPS, 1 SERVING

⅔ cup water

1 cup fresh or thawed frozen peach slices

2 apples, unpeeled and chopped

½ cup chopped romaine lettuce

½ cup chopped kale, packed

EQUIPMENT

measuring cups

cutting board

chef's knife, 8-inch

blender

rubber spatula

Put all the ingredients in a blender and process on high speed until smooth. Stored in a sealed jar in the refrigerator, Peachy Apple Green Smoothie will keep for 24 hours.

Per serving: calories: 145, protein: 3 g, fat: 1 g, carbohydrate: 29 g, fiber: 6 g, sodium: 18 mg

Fresh mint adds a fragrant twist to this basic green smoothie.

minty green smoothie

YIELD: 2½ CUPS, 1 SERVING

⅔ cup water

2 apples, unpeeled and chopped

1 orange, peeled, sectioned, and seeded

2 cups chopped Swiss chard or bok choy, packed

½ cup mint leaves, packed

EQUIPMENT

measuring cups

cutting board

chef's knife, 8-inch

blender

rubber spatula

Put all the ingredients in a blender and process on high speed until smooth. Stored in a sealed jar in the refrigerator, Minty Green Smoothie will keep for 12 hours.

Per serving: calories: 197, protein: 3 g, fat: 1 g, carbohydrate: 41 g, fiber: 10 g, sodium: 157 mg

This meal in a glass will nourish you with antioxidant-rich berries, dark leafy greens, omega-3 fatty acids, and protein.

creamy berry green smoothie

YIELD: 2½ CUPS, 2 SERVINGS

¾ cup water

½ cup **Hemp Milk** (page 57) **or Coconut Milk** (page 59)

1 cup frozen mixed berries

½ banana

1½ cups chopped Swiss chard, packed

1½ cups chopped kale, packed

1 tablespoon ground flaxseeds

1 tablespoon raw vegan protein powder (see Glossary, page 201; optional)

2 drops liquid stevia (optional)

EQUIPMENT

measuring cups

cutting board

chef's knife

measuring spoons

blender

rubber spatula

Put all the ingredients in a blender and process on high speed until smooth. Serve immediately.

Per serving: calories: 220, protein: 9 g, fat: 8 g, carbohydrate: 25 g, fiber: 10 g, sodium: 86 mg

Pineapple lets you increase the amount of bitter greens (which are the most nutritious ones) without compromising sweet flavor.

pineapple green smoothie

YIELD: 3 CUPS, 2 SERVINGS

⅔ cup water

2 cups chopped fresh pineapple

1½ cups chopped kale, collard greens, or dandelion greens, packed

EQUIPMENT

measuring cups

cutting board

chef's knife, 8-inch

blender

rubber spatula

Put all the ingredients in a blender and process on high speed until smooth. Serve immediately.

Per serving: calories: 103, protein: 3 g, fat: 1 g, carbohydrate: 22 g, fiber: 3 g, sodium: 23 mg

Grapes provide health-supportive phytonutrients and a sweet-tart flavor.

banana-grape green smoothie

YIELD: 4 CUPS, 2 SERVINGS

¼ cup water

2 cups red seedless grapes

2 bananas

3 cups chopped Swiss chard or kale, packed

EQUIPMENT

measuring cups

blender

rubber spatula

Put all the ingredients in a blender and process on high speed until smooth. Serve immediately.

Per serving: calories: 223, protein: 3 g, fat: 1 g, carbohydrate: 52 g, fiber: 5 g, sodium: 119 mg

Can you enjoy vitamin-rich collard greens raw? Sure! The mango makes this smoothie mild, sweet, and creamy.

mango and collard greens smoothie

YIELD: 2 CUPS, 1 SERVING

2 cups fresh or thawed frozen mango chunks

1 cup chopped collard greens, packed

EQUIPMENT

cutting board

chef's knife, 8-inch

measuring cups

blender

rubber spatula

Put all the ingredients in a blender and process on high speed until smooth. Stored in a sealed jar in the refrigerator, Mango and Collard Greens Smoothie will keep for 12 hours.

Per serving: calories: 225, protein: 3 g, fat: 1 g, carbohydrate: 51 g, fiber: 7 g, sodium: 14 mg

This smoothie is bright, fresh, and vibrant, in both color and taste.

honeydew green smoothie

SEE PHOTO ON FRONT COVER.

YIELD: 2 CUPS, 1 SERVING

½ medium honeydew melon, seeded

2 cups chopped romaine lettuce

EQUIPMENT

cutting board

chef's knife, 8-inch

spoon

measuring cups

blender

rubber spatula

Scoop out the honeydew flesh and put it in a blender. Add the romaine and process on high speed until smooth. Serve immediately.

Per serving: calories: 249, protein: 5 g, fat: 1 g, carbohydrate: 55 g, fiber: 7 g, sodium: 124 mg

Parsley isn't just a garnish anymore. This nutrient-rich herb aids digestion and freshens breath—so use it by the handful and enjoy its bright green color and slightly peppery taste.

pear and parsley green smoothie

SEE PHOTO ON FRONT COVER.   YIELD: 2 CUPS, 2 SERVINGS

⅔ cup water

2 pears, chopped

1 cup chopped fresh
   parsley, packed

EQUIPMENT

measuring cups

cutting board

chef's knife, 8-inch

blender

rubber spatula

Put all the ingredients in a blender and process on high speed until smooth. Stored in a sealed jar in the refrigerator, Pear and Parsley Green Smoothie will keep for 24 hours.

Per serving: calories: 109, protein: 2 g, fat: 1 g, carbohydrate: 22 g, fiber: 5 g, sodium: 17 mg

There is no need to cook cranberries or add sugar to them. Their tartness is perfectly balanced by the sweet pears and grapes in this smoothie.

fall green smoothie

YIELD: 2 CUPS, 1 SERVING

⅔ cup water

1 pear or apple, unpeeled
   and chopped

½ cup fresh cranberries or
   raspberries

½ cup red seedless grapes

1½ cups chopped kale,
   packed

EQUIPMENT

measuring cups

cutting board

chef's knife, 8-inch

blender

rubber spatula

Put all the ingredients in a blender and process on high speed until smooth. Stored in a sealed jar in the refrigerator, Fall Green Smoothie will keep for 24 hours.

Per serving: calories: 226, protein: 5 g, fat: 2 g, carbohydrate: 46 g, fiber: 9 g, sodium: 46 mg

Not in the mood for a sweet-tasting breakfast? This vegetable-rich drink is savory, and it works well for lunch or dinner too.

garden vegetable green smoothie

YIELD: 4 CUPS, 2 SERVINGS

1 cup water

½ zucchini, unpeeled and chopped

½ cucumber, unpeeled and chopped

1 tomato, chopped

2 stalks celery, chopped

½ apple, unpeeled and chopped

2 cups chopped Swiss chard, bok choy, or spinach, packed

¼ lemon, peeled

EQUIPMENT

measuring cups

cutting board

chef's knife, 8-inch

measuring spoons

blender

rubber spatula

Put all the ingredients in a blender and process on high speed until smooth. Stored in a sealed jar in the refrigerator, Garden Vegetable Green Smoothie will keep for 12 hours.

Per serving: calories: 64, protein: 3 g, fat: 1 g, carbohydrate: 11 g, fiber: 4 g, sodium: 123 mg

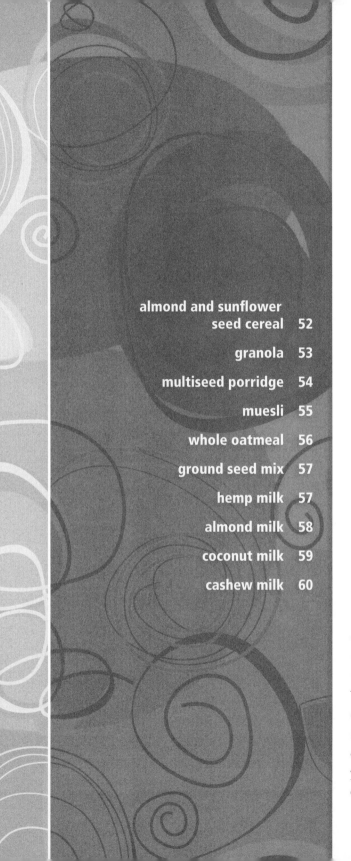

CEREALS AND MILKS

Cereal is America's most popular breakfast food. Unfortunately, most boxed versions are made from refined flour and sugar and have little nutritional value. The recipes in this section use nuts, seeds, and whole grains, and they pack in more flavor than their commercial counterparts. Most recipes suggest serving raw cereals with homemade Almond Milk (page 58), but you may substitute Cashew Milk (page 60), Hemp Milk (page 57), or soy milk if you prefer.

Go nuts—for breakfast.

almond and sunflower seed cereal

YIELD: 1 SERVING

2 tablespoons soaked almonds (see page 7)

2 tablespoons soaked sunflower seeds (see page 7)

1 tablespoon soaked walnuts or pecans (see page 7; optional)

½ cup chopped or sliced fresh fruit (such as apple, banana, berries, kiwifruit, mango, peach, or pineapple)

½ cup Almond Milk (page 58)

EQUIPMENT

measuring spoons

small bowl

cutting board

chef's knife, 8-inch

paring knife

measuring cups

Combine the almonds, sunflower seeds, optional walnuts, and fruit in a small bowl. Serve immediately with the Almond Milk.

Per serving: calories: 281, protein: 9 g, fat: 21 g, carbohydrate: 16 g, fiber: 8 g, sodium: 1 mg

This granola contains no refined sugar or oil, yet it has all the sweetness and crunch of the conventional cereal.

granola

YIELD: 1 CUP, 2 SERVINGS

¼ **cup soaked almonds** (see page 7)

¼ **cup soaked sunflower seeds** (see page 7)

¼ **cup soaked walnuts or pecans** (see page 7)

4 pitted medjool dates, chopped, unsoaked

¼ **teaspoon ground cinnamon**

Dash salt

½ **cup chopped or sliced fresh fruit** (such as apple, banana, berries, kiwifruit, mango, peach, or pineapple)

½ **cup Almond Milk** (page 58)

EQUIPMENT

measuring cups

food processor

measuring spoons

rubber spatula

small bowl

cutting board

chef's knife, 8-inch

paring knife

Put the almonds, sunflower seeds, and walnuts in a food processor fitted with the S blade and pulse briefly, just until coarsely chopped. Add the dates, cinnamon, and salt and process briefly to mix. Stored in a sealed container in the refrigerator, Granola will keep for 2 days. Just before serving, transfer to a small bowl and add the fresh fruit. Serve immediately with the Almond Milk.

RAISIN OR FIG GRANOLA: Replace the medjool dates with ¼ cup of raisins or chopped dried figs, unsoaked.

Per serving: calories: 352, protein: 9 g, fat: 24 g, carbohydrate: 28 g, fiber: 7 g, sodium: 4 mg

This grain-free porridge is the most delicious way I know to get your daily allowance of omega-3 fatty acids and fiber.

multiseed porridge

YIELD: 1 SERVING

3 tablespoons Ground Seed Mix (page 57)

Dash ground cinnamon

¼ **cup Hemp Milk** (page 57), **plus more for serving**

1 teaspoon maple syrup or agave nectar (optional)

¼ **cup chopped or sliced fresh fruit** (such as apple, banana, or berries), **or 2 tablespoons raisins or chopped dates**

EQUIPMENT

measuring spoons

small bowl

whisk

cutting board

chef's knife, 8-inch

paring knife

measuring cups

Put the Ground Seed Mix and cinnamon in a small bowl. Gradually add the Hemp Milk and whisk to combine. Stir in the maple syrup if desired. Serve immediately with additional Hemp Milk and fresh or dried fruit.

Per serving: calories: 199, protein: 10 g, fat: 12 g, carbohydrate: 11 g, fiber: 3 g, sodium: 6 mg

Make a large batch (see note) of this cereal so it will be ready when a sweet craving strikes.

muesli

SEE PHOTO FACING PAGE 24.

YIELD: 1 SERVING

⅓ cup old-fashioned rolled oats

2 tablespoons raisins, unsoaked

1 tablespoon chopped almonds, walnuts, or pecans, unsoaked

2 teaspoons sunflower or pumpkin seeds, unsoaked

2 teaspoons maple syrup, whole cane sugar, or coconut sugar (optional)

½ cup Almond Milk (page 58), or ¼ cup Strawberry Cashew Yogurt (page 36)

¼ cup fresh blueberries or sliced strawberries

EQUIPMENT

measuring cups

measuring spoons

cutting board

chef's knife, 8-inch

small bowl

spoon

Put the oats, raisins, almonds, sunflower seeds, and optional maple syrup in a small bowl. Toss gently to combine. Serve with the Almond Milk and berries.

NOTES

- Stored in a sealed container in the pantry, Muesli will keep for 3 months. If you will be storing it and want to include a sweetener, use whole cane sugar or coconut sugar instead of maple syrup. Alternatively, add the maple syrup just before serving.

- For soft Muesli, soak in ¼ cup of water for 8 to 12 hours at room temperature. Serve with the Almond Milk and berries.

- For a large batch: Increase the amounts to 3 cups of rolled oats, 1 cup of raisins, ½ cup of chopped almonds, ¼ cup of sunflower seeds, and ¼ cup of optional whole cane sugar. Yield: 4 cups, 8 servings.

Per serving: calories: 374, protein: 11 g, fat: 18 g, carbohydrate: 43 g, fiber: 9 g, sodium: 5 mg

Warm up on cool mornings with this comforting breakfast.

whole oatmeal

1 cup soaked oat groats (see note)

½ apple, peeled and chopped

1 tablespoon water

2 teaspoons maple syrup or agave nectar

¼ teaspoon ground cinnamon

¼ teaspoon vanilla extract (optional)

⅛ teaspoon salt

½ cup Almond Milk (page 58)

2 tablespoons raisins, soaked in water for 10 minutes and drained, or 2 tablespoons Dried Fruit Compote (page 30)

EQUIPMENT

measuring cups

cutting board

peeler

chef's knife, 8 inch

measuring spoons

food processor

rubber spatula

small bowl

small colander or fine-mesh strainer

small saucepan (optional)

Put the oat groats, apple, water, maple syrup, cinnamon, optional vanilla extract, and salt in a food processor fitted with the S blade and process until smooth, stopping occasionally to scrape down the work bowl with a rubber spatula. Serve immediately with the Almond Milk and raisins.

NOTE: To make 1 cup of soaked oat groats, put ¾ cup of whole oat groats in a small bowl and cover with water. Let soak for 8 to 12 hours at room temperature. Drain in a fine-mesh strainer and rinse well. Return the groats to the bowl and add enough fresh water to cover. Let soak for 8 to 12 more hours. Drain and rinse again. Stored in a sealed container in the refrigerator, soaked oat groats will keep for 3 days.

WARMING OPTION: Put in a small saucepan over low heat and warm gently for 2 to 3 minutes before adding the Almond Milk and raisins.

Per serving: calories: 264, protein: 11 g, fat: 9 g, carbohydrate: 57 g, fiber: 8 g, sodium: 136 mg

Mango Salsa, *page 77*

Hummus Sandwich, *page 126*

Ground Seed Mix is rich in fiber, protein, and omega-3 fatty acids. Keep it on hand to sprinkle on salads, blend into smoothies, or make Multiseed Porridge (page 54).

ground seed mix

YIELD: 1½ CUPS

½ cup flaxseeds, unsoaked

¼ cup sunflower, pumpkin, or sesame seeds, unsoaked

¼ cup chia seeds or hempseeds, unsoaked

EQUIPMENT

measuring cups

coffee grinder

Put all the seeds in a coffee grinder and process into a fine powder (you may need to do this in two batches). Stored in a sealed container in the refrigerator, Ground Seed Mix will keep for 3 months.

Per 3 tablespoons: calories: 104, protein: 4 g, fat: 7 g, carbohydrate: 5 g, fiber: 2 g, sodium: 1 mg

Hemp milk takes only minutes to make, since hempseeds don't need to be soaked.

hemp milk

YIELD: 2 CUPS, 4 SERVINGS

1½ cups water

½ cup hempseeds, unsoaked

2 teaspoons maple syrup or agave nectar

½ teaspoon vanilla extract (optional)

EQUIPMENT

measuring cups

measuring spoons

blender

rubber spatula

Put the water, hempseeds, maple syrup, and optional vanilla extract in a blender. Process on high speed until smooth. Stored in a sealed container in the refrigerator, Hemp Milk will keep for 5 days. It tends to separate, so shake well before using.

Per serving: calories: 169, protein: 11 g, fat: 10 g, carbohydrate: 10 g, fiber: 1 g, sodium: 10 mg

Homemade Almond Milk is more nutritious than commercial versions, and it takes only minutes to make.

almond milk

YIELD: 2½ CUPS, 4 SERVINGS

2½ cups water

1½ cups soaked almonds (see page 7)

3 pitted medjool dates, soaked in water for 10 minutes and drained

½ teaspoon vanilla extract (optional)

EQUIPMENT

measuring cups

small bowl

measuring spoons

blender

fine-mesh strainer or mesh bag

large bowl

rubber spatula

Put 1½ cups of the water and all the almonds, dates, and optional vanilla extract in a blender. Process on high speed until smooth. Add the remaining cup of water and process on high speed until smooth.

Put a fine-mesh strainer over a large bowl and pour the almond mixture through it. Stir and press the pulp with a rubber spatula to extract as much milk as possible. Discard the pulp. Alternatively, use a mesh bag to strain the milk. Stored in a sealed container in the refrigerator, Almond Milk will keep for 5 days. It tends to separate, so shake well before using.

ALMOND CREAM: Decrease the amount of water to 2 cups. Follow the directions for Almond Milk, but add only ½ cup of water at the end of the blending process.

ALMOND MILK WITH STEVIA: Omit the dates and add 2 drops of liquid stevia. (A naturally sweet herb, stevia can be used if you are avoiding fruit sugar and other sweeteners.)

BRAZIL NUT MILK: Replace the almonds with 1½ cups of soaked Brazil nuts (see page 7), which are a rich source of selenium.

CHOCOLATE ALMOND MILK: After straining the milk, return it to the blender and add ¼ cup of unsweetened cocoa powder and 1½ tablespoons of maple syrup or agave nectar. Process on high speed until well combined. Yield: 3 cups, 4 servings.

SESAME MILK: Replace the almonds with 1½ cups of soaked unhulled sesame seeds (see page 7).

Per serving: calories: 154, protein: 5 g, fat: 12 g, carbohydrate: 9 g, fiber: 4 g, sodium: 0 mg
Note: The nutritional values for this recipe are based on the whole-food ingredients, before straining.

The best-tasting coconut milk is the one you make fresh yourself.

coconut milk

YIELD: 2½ CUPS, 4 SERVINGS

2½ cups very hot water

1½ cups unsweetened shredded dried coconut, unsoaked

EQUIPMENT

measuring cups

blender

large bowl

fine-mesh strainer or mesh bag

rubber spatula

Put 1½ cups of the water and the coconut in a blender. Process on high speed until smooth. Add the remaining cup of water and process on high speed until smooth. Let sit for 5 minutes.

Put a fine-mesh strainer over a large bowl and pour the coconut mixture through it. Stir and press the pulp with a rubber spatula to extract as much milk as possible. Discard the pulp. Alternatively, use a mesh bag to strain the milk. Stored in a sealed container in the refrigerator, Coconut Milk will keep for 5 days. It tends to separate, so shake well before using.

LIGHT COCONUT MILK: Add ½ cup of additional hot water.

Per serving: calories: 200, protein: 2 g, fat: 20 g, carbohydrate: 8 g, fiber: 4 g, sodium: 10 mg
Note: The nutritional values for this recipe are based on the whole-food ingredients, before straining.

Cashew Milk is especially quick to make, as it does not need to be strained.

cashew milk

YIELD: 2 CUPS, 4 SERVINGS

1½ cups water

½ **cup soaked cashews** (see page 7)

2 teaspoons maple syrup or agave nectar

½ **teaspoon vanilla extract** (optional)

EQUIPMENT

measuring cups

measuring spoons

blender

rubber spatula

Put the water, cashews, maple syrup, and optional vanilla extract in a blender. Process on high speed until smooth. Stored in a sealed container in the refrigerator, Cashew Milk will keep for 5 days. It tends to separate, so shake well before using.

CASHEW CREAM: Decrease the water to 1 cup. Cashew cream makes a good substitute for dairy cream in coffee or tea.

CHOCOLATE CASHEW MILK: Add 3 tablespoons of unsweetened cocoa powder and an additional 2½ teaspoons of maple syrup.

Per serving: calories: 114, protein: 3 g, fat: 8 g, carbohydrate: 8 g, fiber: 1 g, sodium: 2 mg

EASY SNACKS

Some people feel satisfied with three meals a day, while others need to add a snack or two. Snacks should be quick to prepare and easy to transport.

Fresh raw vegetables are good because they won't spike your blood sugar, are low in calories and high in fiber, and satisfy the urge for crunchy foods. Try Crudités (page 91) when you get the midmorning or midafternoon munchies. I like to make a big batch every couple of days and store it in a container in the refrigerator so I can grab some whenever the urge to snack hits. Enjoy Crudités alone or with a dip, such as Zucchini Hummus (page 70). Alternatively, drink your veggies as a snack. Leftover green vegetable juice from breakfast makes a great afternoon pick-me-up.

Fresh fruit is a delicious and simple snack that will quell the urge for sweets. Enjoy an apple, banana, mango, peach, plum, or tangerine. Or have a fruit smoothie, salad, or platter (see pages 28 to 36) or a green smoothie (see pages 39 to 50).

For more protein, try soaked almonds (page 7) or a few Brazil nuts. Eat them alone or with cucumber slices, or combine them with fresh or dried fruit (such as dates, figs, or goji berries) for a sweet treat.

Macadamia nuts with raisins make a calorie-packed snack that is great when you're hiking. For a more elaborate trail mix, combine 1 cup of nuts and seeds (such as almonds, cashews, pecans, and sunflower seeds), ½ cup of dried fruit (such as chopped apricots, chopped dates, and dark or golden raisins), and a sprinkle of salt.

Almond Butter and Cashew Butter (page 78) are satisfying spreads that can be served with fruits or vegetables. Use nut butter as a dip for carrot, celery, and cucumber slices. Try a banana or a celery stalk spread with nut butter and topped with a few raisins. Or make an apple "sandwich": slice an apple thinly crosswise and remove the seeds and core with a paring knife. Spread one apple slice with nut butter and top with a second slice.

If you prefer five small meals during the day instead of three larger ones, many of the recipes in this book are ideal. At midmorning, try a raw soup or one of the dips with vegetable sticks. When a sweet craving strikes midafternoon, have a guilt-free raw dessert.

MENUS FOR LUNCH AND DINNER

For lunch, rely on classic combinations such as soup and a salad or soup and a sandwich. For an elegant dinner, follow the French custom of serving three small courses. This not only creates an attractive meal but also improves digestion by slowing down the eating process. Start with a small bowl of soup or a small plate of salad. Then present the entrée on its own plate, perhaps with a vegetable side dish, garnish, or sauce. If you are having dessert, serve it on a third small plate or in a small bowl or ramekin. The following pages offer a variety of ways to put it all together.

Sample Lunch Menus

Cream of Tomato Soup (page 81)
Veggie Sub (page 129)

Green Salad with Fennel and Cherry Tomatoes (page 93)
Pizza Sandwich (page 128)

Hummus Sandwich (page 126)
Tabouli (page 152)

Garden Salad (page 94)
Pecan Pâté (page 72)
Sweet Mustard Dressing (page 121)

Greek Salad (page 103)
Garden Wrap (page 133)

California Rolls (page 134)
Cucumber with Fresh Mint (page 144)

Garden Vegetable Soup (page 84)
Crudités (page 91) with Mock Sour Cream and Chive Dip (page 68)

Rainbow Salad (page 96)
Stuffed Tomato with Not Tuna Pâté (page 142)

Papaya-Lime Soup (page 88)
Mango and Avocado Salad (page 109) or Taco Salad (page 99)

Spinach-Apple Soup (page 89)
Caesar Salad (page 95) or The Wedge (page 98)

Sample Dinner Menus

Cream of Zucchini Soup (page 82)
Zucchini Pasta al Pesto or with Marinara Sauce (page 139)
Mediterranean Kale (page 149)
Chocolate Mousse (page 180) with Vanilla Crème Sauce (page 185)

Tricolor Salad (page 111)
Tomato Stack (page 140)
Carrots with Parsley and Walnuts (page 146)
Flourless Chocolate Cake with Fresh Raspberries (page 162)

Green Salad (page 92)
Not Meatballs (page 136)
Coleslaw (page 147) or Dilly Slaw (page 150)
Apple Crisp (page 171)

Jerusalem Salad (page 107)
Stuffed Dates in Marinara Sauce (page 140)
Carrots with Moroccan Spices (page 145)
Almond Cookies (page 164) or Chocolate Pie or Tart with Strawberries (page 177)

Shaved Beet Salad (page 110)
Stuffed Mushroom with Sunflower Seed and Sun-Dried Tomato Pâté (page 138)
Swiss Chard with Pine Nuts and Raisins (page 153)
Blueberry Tart (page 176) or Strawberries with Raspberry Jam (page 34)

Miso Soup (page 86) or Ramen (page 87)

Spring Roll (page 137)

Mango Sorbet (page 192) or Key Lime Mousse (page 179)

Gazpacho (page 85)

Stuffed Bell Pepper with Guacamole (page 142)

Latin American Cabbage (page 148)

Tropical Fruit Pie or Tart (page 173)

lunch and dinner

Raw lunches and dinners need not be limited to salads! For lunch, try one of my blended vegetable soups and a sandwich made with romaine lettuce leaves instead of bread. Or if a salad is what you want, make it more substantial and interesting by topping it with a scoop of Guacamole (page 67), Zucchini Hummus (page 70), or Not Tuna Pâté (page 71). Try beginning dinner with a soup, followed by an entrée with a vegetable side dish, and finishing with a dessert.

If you eat cooked foods, there are many ways to combine them with raw ones. Choose a warm soup, such as vegetable or lentil, or have steamed vegetables, such as asparagus, broccoli, cauliflower, collard greens, or green beans, as side dishes. (For some people, these vegetables are too fibrous to eat raw in large quantities but are easy to digest when lightly cooked.) You may decide to replace a raw entrée with a cooked one or to add cooked foods to your salad or sandwich. Experiment and you will find the right combination for you.

DIPS, PÂTÉS, AND SAVORY SAUCES

All the dips and pâtés in this chapter make delicious appetizers for any party when served with Crudités (page 91). No one will miss the unhealthful mayonnaise-laden versions. Raw dips and pâtés are also versatile staples that you can prepare each week and keep on hand. Pack them along with vegetable sticks for easy-to-transport snacks or light lunches. Use dips and pâtés as satisfying fillings for sandwiches (see pages 125 to 131) and hearty additions to salads. An ice-cream scoop will put a dollop of dip or pâté atop your salad for an attractive presentation. The sauces in this chapter—Marinara Sauce (page 74), Mock Peanut Sauce (page 75), Pesto (page 78), and Olive Tapenade (page 69)—are familiar favorites. These sauces work as flavorful toppings both for savory cooked and raw dishes.

Serve this creamy mayonnaise as a dressing for Dilly Slaw (page 150).

sweet tahini mayonnaise

YIELD: 1 CUP, 4 SERVINGS

½ cup raw tahini

½ cup water, plus more to thin if needed

2 tablespoons freshly squeezed lemon juice

1 tablespoon agave nectar or maple syrup

¼ teaspoon salt

EQUIPMENT

measuring cups

citrus juicer or reamer

measuring spoons

blender

rubber spatula

Put all the ingredients in a blender and process on medium speed until smooth. Stored in a sealed container in the refrigerator, Sweet Tahini Mayonnaise will keep for 3 days. Stir in a little additional water before using, since this sauce will thicken slightly after refrigerating.

Per serving: calories: 188, protein: 5 g, fat: 14 g, carbohydrate: 10 g, fiber: 3 g, sodium: 156 mg

When you have minced onion and crushed garlic on hand, this classic recipe takes five minutes. Serve it with a salad, as a dip with Crudités (page 91), or in a Guacamole Sandwich (page 125).

guacamole

YIELD: ½ CUP, 2 SERVINGS

1 avocado, chopped

1½ teaspoons minced onion

1 teaspoon freshly squeezed lime juice

½ teaspoon crushed garlic

Dash cayenne

Dash salt

EQUIPMENT

cutting board

chef's knife, 8-inch

measuring spoons

citrus juicer or reamer

garlic press

small bowl

fork

Put all the ingredients in a small bowl. Mash with a fork, leaving the mixture slightly chunky. Serve immediately.

Per serving: calories: 146, protein: 2 g, fat: 13 g, carbohydrate: 2 g, fiber: 6 g, sodium: 7 mg

This tastes like ranch dip, only better. Serve it with Crudités (page 91).

mock sour cream and chive dip

SEE PHOTO FACING PAGE 120.

YIELD: 1 CUP, 4 SERVINGS

1 cup soaked cashews (see page 7)

½ cup water

2 tablespoons freshly squeezed lemon juice

½ teaspoon garlic powder

½ teaspoon onion powder

¼ teaspoon salt

2 tablespoons minced fresh chives or green onions

1 tablespoon minced fresh basil, or 1 teaspoon dried

1 tablespoon minced fresh dill, or 1 teaspoon dried
   dill weed

EQUIPMENT

measuring cups

measuring spoons

citrus juicer or reamer

cutting board

chef's knife, 8-inch

blender

rubber spatula

Put the cashews, water, lemon juice, garlic powder, onion powder, and salt in a blender and process on high speed until smooth, stopping occasionally to scrape down the blender jar with a rubber spatula. Add the chives, basil, and dill and pulse briefly to mix. Cover and refrigerate for at least 30 minutes before serving. Stored in a sealed container in the refrigerator, Mock Sour Cream and Chive Dip will keep for 5 days.

Per serving: calories: 213, protein: 7 g, fat: 17 g, carbohydrate: 11 g, fiber: 1 g, sodium: 5 mg

This spread is easy to make yet has a complex, "gourmet" flavor. Use Olive Tapenade as a filling for any sandwich or as a salad dressing.

olive tapenade

YIELD: ½ CUP, 4 SERVINGS

1 cup pitted black or green olives

2 tablespoons capers

4 teaspoons extra-virgin olive oil

2 teaspoons freshly squeezed lemon juice

1½ teaspoons minced fresh basil, or ½ teaspoon dried

1 teaspoon crushed garlic

Dash ground pepper

EQUIPMENT

measuring cups

measuring spoons

citrus juicer or reamer

garlic press

cutting board

chef's knife, 8-inch

food processor

rubber spatula

Put all the ingredients in a food processor fitted with the S blade and process until smooth, stopping occasionally to scrape down the work bowl with a rubber spatula. Stored in a sealed container in the refrigerator, Olive Tapenade will keep for 5 days.

SUN-DRIED TOMATO TAPENADE: Replace the olives with soaked or oil-packed sun-dried tomatoes. Omit the capers.

Per serving: calories: 106, protein: 1 g, fat: 10 g, carbohydrate: 3 g, fiber: 1 g, sodium: 381 mg

Zucchini Hummus is lighter than the traditional bean version, but it tastes just as delicious. Serve it with a salad, as a dip with Crudités (page 91), or in a Hummus Sandwich (page 126).

zucchini hummus

SEE PHOTO FACING PAGE 57.

YIELD: 1 CUP, 2 SERVINGS

1½ **cups peeled and chopped zucchini** (about 1 zucchini)

2 **tablespoons raw tahini**

2 **tablespoons freshly squeezed lemon juice**

½ **teaspoon crushed garlic**

¼ **teaspoon ground cumin**

¼ **teaspoon paprika**

¼ **teaspoon salt**

EQUIPMENT

cutting board

peeler

chef's knife, 8-inch

measuring cups

measuring spoons

citrus juicer or reamer

garlic press

food processor

rubber spatula

Put all the ingredients in a food processor fitted with the S blade and process until smooth, stopping occasionally to scrape down the work bowl with a rubber spatula. Stored in a sealed container in the refrigerator, Zucchini Hummus will keep for 5 days.

GARBANZO BEAN HUMMUS: Replace the zucchini with 1¼ cups of cooked garbanzo beans and add ¼ cup of water.

Per serving: calories: 107, protein: 4 g, fat: 7 g, carbohydrate: 6 g, fiber: 3 g, sodium: 288 mg

This pâté is my daily staple—it's delicious, versatile, and filling. Not Tuna Pâté is the perfect addition to turn a salad into a main dish. You can also use it as a filling for Not Tuna Rolls (page 134), a Tomato Stack (page 140), a Stuffed Bell Pepper (page 142), or a Not Tuna Sandwich (page 125). You may wish to make a larger batch, since it will keep for five days.

not tuna pâté

SEE PHOTO FACING PAGE 152.   YIELD: ¾ CUP, 2 SERVINGS

½ **cup soaked sunflower seeds** (see page 7)

¼ **cup soaked almonds** (see page 7)

2 tablespoons water

1 tablespoon freshly squeezed lemon juice

¼ **teaspoon salt**

1½ **tablespoons minced celery**

1 tablespoon minced onion

1 tablespoon minced fresh parsley

EQUIPMENT

measuring cups

measuring spoons

citrus juicer or reamer

food processor

rubber spatula

small bowl

cutting board

chef's knife, 8-inch

Put the sunflower seeds, almonds, water, lemon juice, and salt in a food processor fitted with the S blade and process into a paste, stopping occasionally to scrape down the work bowl with a rubber spatula. Transfer to a small bowl and stir in the celery, onion, and parsley until well combined. Stored in a sealed container in the refrigerator, Not Tuna Pâté will keep for 5 days.

NOT SALMON PÂTÉ: Add ¼ cup of shredded carrot to the food processor along with the sunflower seeds, almonds, water, lemon juice, and salt. Replace the parsley with 1 tablespoon of minced fresh dill or 1 teaspoon of dried dill weed.

Per serving: calories: 227, protein: 8 g, fat: 20 g, carbohydrate: 9 g, fiber: 4 g, sodium: 275 mg

This rich, meaty pâté is a good choice when you are really hungry. For a satisfying lunch, have a scoop of it on a Garden Salad (page 94) along with Creamy Tomato Dressing (page 118) or Sweet Mustard Dressing (page 121). You can also serve it in a Walnut Pâté Sandwich (page 127) or a Tomato Stack (page 140), or make it into Not Meatballs (page 136).

walnut pâté

YIELD: ¾ CUP, 2 SERVINGS

1 cup soaked walnuts (see page 7)

1 tablespoon freshly squeezed lemon juice

1 teaspoon extra-virgin olive oil

1 teaspoon tamari

¼ teaspoon garlic powder

Dash salt

1 tablespoon minced onion

1 tablespoon minced fresh parsley

EQUIPMENT

measuring cups

citrus juicer or reamer

measuring spoons

food processor

rubber spatula

small bowl

cutting board

chef's knife, 8-inch

Put the walnuts, lemon juice, oil, tamari, garlic powder, and salt in a food processor fitted with the S blade and process into a paste, stopping occasionally to scrape down the work bowl with a rubber spatula. Transfer to a small bowl. Stir in the onion and parsley until well combined. Stored in a sealed container in the refrigerator, Walnut Pâté will keep for 5 days.

CURRIED WALNUT PÂTÉ: Add ¼ teaspoon of curry powder.

PECAN PÂTÉ: Replace the walnuts with 1 cup of soaked pecans (see page 7).

Per serving (6 tablespoons): calories: 325, protein: 7 g, fat: 32 g, carbohydrate: 5 g, fiber: 3 g, sodium: 209 mg

This light, delicately flavored pâté tastes great in a Stuffed Mushroom (page 138) or a Stuffed Bell Pepper (page 142). Add sun-dried tomatoes (see variation) for an Italian flavor.

sunflower seed–herb pâté

YIELD: ¾ CUP, 2 SERVINGS

1 cup soaked sunflower seeds (see page 7)

2 tablespoons water

1 tablespoon freshly squeezed lemon juice

½ teaspoon crushed garlic

¼ teaspoon salt

Dash cayenne or ground pepper

1 tablespoon minced red or green onion

2 teaspoons minced fresh dill, basil, or parsley

EQUIPMENT

measuring cups

measuring spoons

citrus juicer or reamer

garlic press

food processor

rubber spatula

small bowl

cutting board

chef's knife, 8-inch

Put the sunflower seeds, water, lemon juice, garlic, salt, and cayenne in a food processor fitted with the S blade and process into a paste, stopping occasionally to scrape down the work bowl with a rubber spatula. Transfer to a small bowl. Stir in the onion and dill until well combined. Stored in a sealed container in the refrigerator, Sunflower Seed–Herb Pâté will keep for 5 days.

PUMPKIN SEED–HERB PÂTÉ: Replace the sunflower seeds with soaked pumpkin seeds (see page 7).

SUNFLOWER SEED AND SUN-DRIED TOMATO PÂTÉ: Add ⅓ cup of soaked or oil-packed sun-dried tomatoes to the food processor along with the sunflower seeds, water, lemon juice, garlic, salt, and cayenne.

SEE PHOTO BETWEEN PAGES 152 AND 153.

Per serving: calories: 156, protein: 6 g, fat: 14 g, carbohydrate: 6 g, fiber: 2 g, sodium: 136 mg

This tastes like the best slow-simmered tomato sauce you've ever had. Serve it over Zucchini Pasta (page 139) or Not Meatballs (page 136).

marinara sauce

SEE PHOTO FACING PAGE 89.

YIELD: 1 CUP, 3 SERVINGS

½ cup chopped tomato

½ cup sun-dried tomatoes, soaked or oil-packed

½ red bell pepper, chopped

1 tablespoon minced fresh basil, or 1 teaspoon dried

1 tablespoon extra-virgin olive oil

1 teaspoon dried oregano

½ teaspoon crushed garlic

¼ teaspoon plus ⅛ teaspoon salt

Dash cayenne

Dash ground pepper (optional)

EQUIPMENT

cutting board

serrated knife, 5-inch

chef's knife, 8-inch

measuring cups

measuring spoons

garlic press

food processor

rubber spatula

Put all the ingredients in a food processor fitted with the S blade and process until smooth, stopping occasionally to scrape down the work bowl with a rubber spatula. Stored in a sealed container in the refrigerator, Marinara Sauce will keep for 3 days.

MIDDLE EASTERN MARINARA SAUCE: Include the optional ground pepper and add a dash of ground cardamom, ground cinnamon, and ground cumin.

PUTTANESCA SAUCE: Increase the cayenne to ⅛ teaspoon. Stir 2 tablespoons of thinly sliced black olives into the finished sauce.

Per serving: calories: 77, protein: 2 g, fat: 5 g, carbohydrate: 6 g, fiber: 2 g, sodium: 193 mg

Peanut butter is made from roasted, not raw, peanuts, so I use raw almond butter for this tasty sauce. Try it as a dip for a Spring Roll (page 137).

mock peanut sauce

YIELD: 1 CUP, 4 SERVINGS

½ cup raw almond butter (preferably homemade, page 78)

¼ cup water

1 tablespoon freshly squeezed lemon juice

2 teaspoons maple syrup or agave nectar

2 teaspoons tamari

½ teaspoon crushed garlic

¼ teaspoon minced fresh ginger

Dash cayenne

Dash salt

EQUIPMENT

measuring cups

citrus juicer or reamer

measuring spoons

garlic press

file grater

blender

rubber spatula

Put all the ingredients in a blender and process on medium speed until smooth. Stored in a sealed container in the refrigerator, Mock Peanut Sauce will keep for 5 days.

Per serving: calories: 149, protein: 6 g, fat: 12 g, carbohydrate: 8 g, fiber: 3 g, sodium: 205 mg

With a food processor, homemade salsa is easy to make. Try it on top of a green salad; it's so juicy, you won't need additional dressing.

salsa

YIELD: ½ CUP, 1 SERVING

2 Roma tomatoes, seeded and quartered

1½ teaspoons minced fresh cilantro

1½ teaspoons minced red or green onion

½ teaspoon freshly squeezed lime juice

¼ teaspoon minced jalapeño chile, or dash cayenne

¼ teaspoon crushed garlic

⅛ teaspoon salt

EQUIPMENT

cutting board

serrated knife, 5-inch

chef's knife, 8-inch

food processor

rubber spatula

measuring spoons

citrus juicer or reamer

garlic press

Put the tomatoes in a food processor fitted with the S blade and pulse a few times to chop, stopping occasionally to scrape down the work bowl with a rubber spatula. Do not overprocess. Add the cilantro, onion, lime juice, chile, garlic, and salt and pulse briefly, just to mix. Let sit for 10 minutes before serving to allow the flavors to meld. Serve immediately.

Per serving: calories: 54, protein: 2 g, fat: 1 g, carbohydrate: 9 g, fiber: 3 g, sodium: 300 mg

Homemade fruit salsa is a succulent summer treat.

mango salsa

SEE PHOTO FACING PAGE 56.

YIELD: 2 CUPS, 4 SERVINGS

1 mango, peeled and diced

2 Roma tomatoes, seeded and diced

1 avocado, diced

½ cucumber, peeled, seeded, and diced

2 tablespoons minced red onion

1 tablespoon minced fresh cilantro

1 teaspoon freshly squeezed lemon or lime juice

¼ teaspoon minced jalapeño chile, or dash cayenne

⅛ teaspoon salt

EQUIPMENT

cutting board

serrated knife, 5-inch

chef's knife, 8-inch

peeler

spoon

measuring spoons

citrus juicer or reamer

medium bowl

rubber spatula

Put all the ingredients in a medium bowl and toss to combine. Let stand for 10 minutes so the flavors blend. Serve immediately.

PEACH SALSA: Replace the mango with 1 peach or nectarine.

PINEAPPLE SALSA: Replace the mango with ¾ cup of diced pineapple.

Per serving: calories: 127, protein: 2 g, fat: 7 g, carbohydrate: 12 g, fiber: 5 g, sodium: 78 mg

Raw almond butter can be purchased at most natural food stores, but homemade is more economical.

almond butter

SEE PHOTO FACING PAGE 25.   YIELD: ¾ CUP

1 cup almonds, unsoaked

Dash salt

EQUIPMENT

measuring cups

food processor

rubber spatula

Put the almonds and salt in a food processor fitted with the S blade and process for 5 to 10 minutes, or until the almonds are ground into a paste, stopping occasionally to scrape down the work bowl with a rubber spatula. Stored in a sealed container in the refrigerator, Almond Butter will keep for 3 months.

CASHEW BUTTER: Replace the almonds with 1 cup of raw unsoaked cashews.

Per 2 tablespoons: calories: 137, protein: 5 g, fat: 12 g, carbohydrate: 5 g, fiber: 3 g, sodium: 22 mg

This aromatic sauce gives meals an authentic Italian flavor. It's delicious as an ingredient in Zucchini Pasta al Pesto (page 139), Pesto Dressing (page 119), or a Tomato Stack (page 140). If you eat cooked food, try Pesto over whole-grain pasta.

pesto

SEE PHOTO FACING PAGE 152.   YIELD: 1 CUP, 6 SERVINGS

2 cups basil leaves, stemmed and firmly packed

¼ cup extra-virgin olive oil

1 teaspoon crushed garlic

¼ teaspoon plus ⅛ teaspoon salt

¼ cup pine nuts, walnuts, or pecans

EQUIPMENT

measuring cups

garlic press

measuring spoons

food processor

rubber spatula

Put the basil, oil, garlic, and salt in a food processor fitted with the S blade and process until the basil is chopped. Add the pine nuts and process until smooth, stopping occasionally to scrape down the work bowl with a rubber spatula. Do not overprocess; flecks of pine nuts should be visible throughout. Stored in a sealed container in the refrigerator, Pesto will keep for 5 days.

Per serving: calories: 129, protein: 1 g, fat: 14 g, carbohydrate: 1 g, fiber: 0 g, sodium: 136 mg

SOUPS

If you get tired of chewing salad, raw soups are an excellent alternative. They're especially nutritious because blending concentrates a large amount of vegetables into a small volume. Blending also helps break down the fiber in vegetables, making them easier to digest, which is particularly important if you are new to raw food. The best raw soups are delicately flavored—not too salty, spicy, or rich—so that you can easily eat a whole bowlful. Fruit soups make a refreshing summer meal, and vegetable soups, served at room temperature or warm, can be eaten year-round. To warm vegetable soup, pour it into a small saucepan and warm over low heat for two to three minutes, taking care not to overheat it.

A blended raw vegetable soup should contain the following components: water, vegetables, fat, citrus juice, seasonings, and salt. The vegetables should be soft, such as cucumber, greens, red bell pepper, tomato, or zucchini. I avoid root and cruciferous vegetables in these soup recipes. Roots, such as beets and carrots, become grainy when blended; and cruciferous vegetables, such as broccoli, cabbage, and collard greens, are too strongly flavored. The best fat to use is avocado—it gets creamy when blended and adds richness without heaviness. For citrus juice, choose lemon, lime, or orange. Seasonings can include garlic, onion, cayenne, fresh or dried herbs, salt, and miso, which adds a deep flavor similar to stock.

Begin making your raw soup by blending the water and the softest vegetables. If you prefer thick soup, use less water. Don't add too much lemon, salt, cayenne, or garlic; you can always spice up the soup later. Add the avocado, fresh herbs, and greens last, to avoid overblending them. Garnish raw soup with a drizzle of Ranch Dressing (page 122) or a sprinkle of minced fresh herbs. For the best flavor, serve immediately. A chilled soup should be refrigerated for thirty minutes before serving. If you want to take the soup with you, transfer it to a Mason jar. It will keep for six hours at room temperature.

Lettuce isn't just for salads. Blending it with cucumber makes a light and delicious soup.

cream of cucumber soup

YIELD: 2 CUPS, 2 SERVINGS

1½ cups chopped romaine lettuce

1 cucumber, peeled, seeded, and chopped

½ cup water

1 tablespoon freshly squeezed lemon juice

½ teaspoon crushed garlic

¼ teaspoon salt

½ avocado, chopped

2 teaspoons extra-virgin olive oil

1 tablespoon minced fresh herbs (dill, fresh mint, tarragon, or cilantro), or 1 teaspoon dried

EQUIPMENT

cutting board

chef's knife, 8-inch

measuring cups

peeler

spoon

citrus juicer or reamer

measuring spoons

garlic press

blender

rubber spatula

Put the lettuce, cucumber, water, lemon juice, garlic, and salt in a blender and process on medium speed until smooth. Add the avocado and oil and process on medium speed until smooth. Add the herbs and process on medium speed briefly, just to mix. Stored in a sealed container in the refrigerator, Cream of Cucumber Soup will keep for 2 days.

Per serving: calories: 145, protein: 2 g, fat: 11 g, carbohydrate: 7 g, fiber: 5 g, sodium: 277 mg

For an all-American soup-and-sandwich lunch, pair Cream of Tomato with a Veggie Sub (page 129).

cream of tomato soup

SEE PHOTO FACING PAGE 88.

YIELD: 1½ CUPS, 2 SERVINGS

3 tomatoes, chopped

¼ cup water

½ teaspoon crushed garlic

¼ teaspoon onion powder

¼ teaspoon salt

½ avocado, chopped

2 teaspoons extra-virgin olive oil

2 teaspoons minced fresh dill or basil, or ½ teaspoon dried

EQUIPMENT

cutting board

serrated knife, 5-inch

chef's knife, 8-inch

measuring cups

garlic press

measuring spoons

blender

rubber spatula

Put the tomatoes, water, garlic, onion powder, and salt in a blender and process on medium speed until smooth. Add the avocado and oil and process on medium speed until smooth. Add the dill and process on medium speed briefly, just to mix. Stored in a sealed container in the refrigerator, Cream of Tomato Soup will keep for 2 days.

Per serving: calories: 153, protein: 3 g, fat: 12 g, carbohydrate: 8 g, fiber: 5 g, sodium: 287 mg

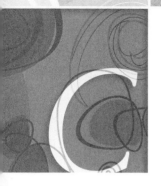

This recipe provides the perfect opportunity to use up those leftover bits of zucchini from Zucchini Pasta (page 139). Serve chilled, at room temperature, or warm (see page 8).

cream of zucchini soup

YIELD: 2 CUPS, 2 SERVINGS

1 zucchini, unpeeled and chopped

1 stalk celery, chopped

¾ cup water, as needed

1 tablespoon freshly squeezed lemon juice

1 teaspoon mellow white miso

½ teaspoon crushed garlic

¼ teaspoon salt

Dash cayenne

½ avocado, chopped

2 teaspoons extra-virgin olive oil

2 teaspoons minced fresh dill, or ½ teaspoon dried dill weed

EQUIPMENT

cutting board

chef's knife, 8-inch

measuring cups

citrus juicer or reamer

measuring spoons

garlic press

blender

rubber spatula

Put the zucchini, celery, ½ cup of the water, lemon juice, miso, garlic, salt, and cayenne in a blender and process on medium speed until smooth. Add the avocado and oil and process on medium speed until smooth. Add the dill and the remaining ¼ cup of water to thin, if necessary, and process on medium speed briefly, just to mix. Stored in a sealed container in the refrigerator, Cream of Zucchini Soup will keep for 2 days.

Per serving: calories: 140, protein: 3 g, fat: 12 g, carbohydrate: 5 g, fiber: 5 g, sodium: 365 mg

Using carrot juice rather than whole carrots makes this soup silky smooth.

curried cream of carrot soup

YIELD: 1½ CUPS, 2 SERVINGS

1 pound carrots, scrubbed and juiced (1 cup juice)

½ avocado, chopped

1 teaspoon freshly squeezed lime juice

¾ teaspoon curry powder

⅛ teaspoon plus 1 pinch salt

1 tablespoon minced fresh cilantro, for garnish

EQUIPMENT

juicer

measuring cups

cutting board

chef's knife, 8-inch

citrus juicer or reamer

measuring spoons

blender

rubber spatula

Put the carrot juice, avocado, lime juice, curry powder, and salt in a blender and process on medium speed until smooth. Garnish with the cilantro. Serve immediately.

Per serving: calories: 168, protein: 3 g, fat: 7 g, carbohydrate: 17 g, fiber: 10 g, sodium: 299 mg

This soup is a green version of Gazpacho (page 85). The basil adds a garden-fresh aroma and flavor.

garden vegetable soup

YIELD: 2 CUPS, 2 SERVINGS

1 zucchini, unpeeled and chopped

¾ cup water, as needed

½ tomato, chopped

1 stalk celery, chopped

1 green onion, chopped

1 tablespoon freshly squeezed lemon juice

1½ teaspoons mellow white miso

½ teaspoon crushed garlic

Dash cayenne

Dash salt

1 cup chopped spinach or Swiss chard, packed

6 leaves basil

½ avocado, chopped

EQUIPMENT

cutting board

chef's knife, 8-inch

measuring cups

citrus juicer or reamer

measuring spoons

garlic press

blender

rubber spatula

Put the zucchini, ½ cup of the water, tomato, celery, green onion, lemon juice, miso, garlic, cayenne, and salt in a blender and process on medium speed until smooth. Add the spinach and basil and process on medium speed until smooth. Add the avocado and process on medium speed until smooth. Add the remaining ¼ cup of water to thin, if necessary, and process on medium speed briefly, just to mix. Stored in a sealed container in the refrigerator, Garden Vegetable Soup will keep for 2 days.

Per serving: calories: 119, protein: 4 g, fat: 7 g, carbohydrate: 7 g, fiber: 6 g, sodium: 211 mg

You won't miss the bread that is often used to thicken this Spanish classic. Blending the vegetables delivers authentic texture.

gazpacho

YIELD: 3 CUPS, 2 SERVINGS

4 tomatoes, chopped

¼ red bell pepper, chopped

¼ cucumber, peeled, seeded, and chopped

½ stalk celery, chopped

1 green onion, chopped

3 tablespoons chopped fresh parsley

1 small radish, sliced (optional)

1½ teaspoons freshly squeezed lime juice

1½ teaspoons extra-virgin olive oil

¼ teaspoon salt

Dash ground pepper

EQUIPMENT

cutting board

chef's knife, 8-inch

serrated knife, 5-inch

peeler

spoon

measuring spoons

citrus juicer or reamer

blender

rubber spatula

Put all the ingredients in a blender and process on medium speed until blended but still a little chunky. Stored in a sealed container in the refrigerator, Gazpacho will keep for 2 days.

Per serving: calories: 97, protein: 3 g, fat: 4 g, carbohydrate: 11 g, fiber: 4 g, sodium: 302 mg

This recipe will satisfy your craving for hot soup during the cold season. The soaked dried mushroom adds a deep, smoky flavor.

miso soup

YIELD: 1⅕ CUPS, 1 SERVING

1 cup plus 2 tablespoons water

¼ cup peeled and thinly sliced carrot

¼ cup baby spinach, firmly packed

1 dried shiitake mushroom, soaked for 30 minutes in warm water, drained, and thinly sliced (optional)

1 tablespoon mellow white miso

1 teaspoon thinly sliced green onion, for garnish

¼ teaspoon toasted sesame oil, for garnish

EQUIPMENT

measuring cups

cutting board

peeler

chef's knife, 8-inch

small bowl

small colander or fine-mesh strainer

small saucepan

measuring spoons

small bowl

fork

wooden spoon

Put 1 cup of the water and the carrot, spinach, and optional mushroom in a small saucepan. Cover and bring to a boil over medium-high heat. Immediately remove from the heat and let stand for 5 minutes. Combine the remaining 2 tablespoons of water with the miso in a small bowl. Whisk with a fork until blended. Add to the water and vegetables and stir to combine. Serve immediately, garnished with the green onion and oil.

Per serving: calories: 136, protein: 4 g, fat: 4 g, carbohydrate: 14 g, fiber: 5 g, sodium: 507 mg

Zucchini noodles are the secret ingredient in this soothing bowl of broth.

ramen

SEE PHOTO FACING PAGE 89.

YIELD: 2½ CUPS, 2 SERVINGS

1 zucchini, peeled

2¼ cups water

½ cup peeled and thinly sliced carrot

½ cup thinly sliced cremini mushrooms

½ cup baby spinach, firmly packed

2 tablespoons mellow white miso

2 teaspoons thinly sliced green onion

¼ teaspoon tamari

Dash salt

EQUIPMENT

peeler

vegetable spiral slicer

measuring cups

cutting board

chef's knife, 8-inch

small saucepan

measuring spoons

small bowl

fork

wooden spoon

Cut the zucchini into thin noodles using a vegetable spiral slicer. Alternatively, use a vegetable peeler to create long ribbons by drawing the peeler down all sides of the zucchini until you reach the core.

Put 2 cups of the water and the carrot, mushrooms, and spinach in a small saucepan. Cover and bring to a boil over medium-high heat. Immediately remove from the heat and let stand for 5 minutes. Combine the remaining ¼ cup of water with the miso in a small bowl. Whisk with a fork until blended. Add the miso mixture, zucchini noodles, green onion, tamari, and salt to the water and vegetables and stir to combine. Serve immediately.

Per serving: calories: 84, protein: 5 g, fat: 1 g, carbohydrate: 11 g, fiber: 4 g, sodium: 300 mg

For a tropical presentation, serve this soup in hollowed-out papaya shells, garnished with diced mango and fresh mint.

papaya-lime soup

SEE PHOTO ON FACING PAGE.

YIELD: 2 CUPS, 2 SERVINGS

1½ cups chopped papaya (about 1 medium papaya; see note)

½ large mango, chopped

2 tablespoons freshly squeezed orange juice

1 tablespoon freshly squeezed lime juice

2 fresh strawberries, hulled

Diced fresh mango, for garnish

4 leaves mint, cut in thin strips, for garnish

EQUIPMENT

cutting board

chef's knife, 8-inch

measuring cups

citrus juicer or reamer

measuring spoons

blender

rubber spatula

Put the papaya, mango, orange juice, lime juice, and strawberries in a blender and process on medium speed until smooth. Serve immediately, garnished with diced mango and the mint.

NOTE: To chop the flesh of a papaya, first cut the fruit in half lengthwise. Scoop the seeds out with a spoon and discard them. Scoop the remaining flesh out of each half and chop coarsely.

Per serving: calories: 88, protein: 1 g, fat: 0 g, carbohydrate: 20 g, fiber: 3 g, sodium: 5 mg

Cream of Tomato Soup, *page 81*, **with drizzle of Ranch Dressing,** *page 122*

Papaya-Lime Soup, *page 88*

Ramen, *page 87*

Zucchini Pasta with Marinara Sauce, *page 139*, **and Not Meatballs,** *page 136*

Fresh apples give sweetness and depth of flavor to this soup.

spinach-apple soup

YIELD: 1½ CUPS, 1 SERVING

2 cups spinach leaves, firmly packed

½ apple, peeled and chopped

¾ cup water, as needed

1 teaspoon freshly squeezed lemon juice

Dash salt

½ avocado, chopped

EQUIPMENT

measuring cups

cutting board

peeler

chef's knife, 8-inch

citrus juicer or reamer

measuring spoons

blender

rubber spatula

Put the spinach, apple, ½ cup of the water, lemon juice, and salt in a blender and process on medium speed until smooth. Add the avocado and process on medium speed until smooth. Add the remaining ¼ of cup water to thin, if necessary, and process on medium speed briefly, just to mix. Stored in a sealed container in the refrigerator, Spinach-Apple Soup will keep for 2 days.

SWISS CHARD AND APPLE SOUP: Replace the spinach with 2 cups of chopped Swiss chard.

Per serving: calories: 200, protein: 5 g, fat: 14 g, carbohydrate: 10 g, fiber: 10 g, sodium: 203 mg

SALADS

Any diet is improved by adding a leafy green salad each day. A great salad begins with fresh organic red or green leaf lettuce, mesclun, romaine lettuce or a combination. One part leaf lettuce or mesclun and one part romaine lettuce is a good mix. Leaf lettuces and mesclun are best used within a few days; I recommend buying smaller amounts twice a week to ensure freshness. Alternatively, since romaine lettuce keeps longer, use it in your salads during the latter part of the week. For crispy romaine salads, remove the wilted outer leaves from the head, or buy romaine hearts, which are often available in convenient packages of three.

For a simple salad, one or two types of lettuce are all you need. For a more elaborate creation, include spicier greens (such as arugula, frisée, mâche, spinach, or watercress), fresh herbs (such as basil, mint, or parsley), and small amounts of thinly sliced vegetables (such as avocado, cabbage, carrot, celery, cucumber, or onion). A mandoline is handy for preparing vegetables such as cabbage, carrots, or onions, which are more palatable in raw salads when sliced ultrathin. Alternatively, small amounts of fruit can be tasty in a simple green salad—think halved grapes or figs, whole raspberries, or thinly sliced pears or strawberries.

To prepare a green salad, first tear all the lettuce into bite-sized pieces and put them in a salad spinner. Add fresh herbs if desired. Fill the spinner with water and swirl the greens around with your hands. Lift out the spinner's insert and pour out the water from the base bowl. Put the insert back into the bowl and spin the greens dry. (You can store the dried greens in the salad spinner in the refrigerator for up to three days.)

Put the lettuce in a large bowl and add any other ingredients. Toss the salad with the dressing of your choice. Serve it directly from the bowl, or for an attractive presentation, arrange individual servings of salad on small plates. You may want to reserve some of the sliced accompaniments to garnish each plate.

To make a salad into a one-dish meal, top it with a scoop of dip or pâté. Or, if you eat cooked foods, add some leftover steamed vegetables (such as asparagus, beets, broccoli, cauliflower, green beans, or sweet potatoes), whole grains, or beans.

If you need to carry a main-dish salad with you during the day, put two tablespoons of dressing in a quart-sized Mason jar. Add one cup of raw or steamed vegetables if desired. Put two cups of lettuce on top of these ingredients, which will absorb the flavor of the dressing and prevent the lettuce from wilting. When you're ready to serve the salad, invert the jar onto a plate. Voilá! The lettuce becomes the base and the marinated ingredients the topping.

"Crudités" is French for cut-up raw veggies. This colorful combination, cut into attractive shapes, works for both a daily snack and a fancy party platter (just increase the quantities as needed). Serve with any dip, sauce, pâté, or salad dressing.

crudités

SEE PHOTO FACING PAGE 120.   YIELD: 1 SERVING

½ carrot, peeled and sliced on the diagonal

½ stalk celery, sliced on the diagonal

¼ cucumber, peeled, seeded, and sliced on the diagonal

½ red bell pepper, cut into 6 chunks

4 broccoli florets

4 cherry tomatoes

EQUIPMENT

cutting board

peeler

spoon

chef's knife, 8-inch

serving plate

Arrange the carrot, celery, cucumber, and bell pepper in a circle on a serving plate and put the broccoli florets and cherry tomatoes in the center. Stored in a sealed container in the refrigerator, Crudités will keep for 3 days.

CRUDITÉS WITH BLANCHED VEGETABLES: Tougher vegetables, such as broccoli, are easier for some people to digest when lightly blanched. To blanch the broccoli, put 4 cups of water in a small saucepan and bring to a boil over high heat. Turn off the heat. Add the broccoli and let sit for 2 minutes. Drain and rinse the broccoli with cold water to stop the cooking. Other vegetables that can be blanched prior to serving as crudités include asparagus, cauliflower, and green beans.

Per serving: calories: 72, protein: 3 g, fat: 1 g, carbohydrate: 12 g, fiber: 4 g, sodium: 64 mg

Sometimes simple is best, especially when the salad will be followed by a more elaborate meal.

green salad

YIELD: 1 SERVING

2 cups torn red leaf, green leaf, or romaine lettuce or mesclun

1 tablespoon Classic Vinaigrette (page 113), **Apple Vinaigrette** (page 113), **Lemon-Herb Dressing** (page 120), **or Sweet Mustard Dressing** (page 121)

4 thin slices Roma tomato, cucumber, or carrot, for garnish

EQUIPMENT

salad spinner

measuring cups

measuring spoons

medium bowl

tongs

serving plate

Put the lettuce and vinaigrette in a medium bowl and toss gently. Transfer to a serving plate. Garnish with the tomato. Serve immediately.

GREEN SALAD WITH BERRIES OR GRAPES: Omit the tomato. Top with ¼ cup of fresh blueberries, raspberries, sliced strawberries, or halved seedless grapes.

GREEN SALAD WITH DRIED FRUITS: Omit the tomato. Top with 1 tablespoon of dried cranberries, dried cherries, sliced medjool dates, or golden or dark raisins. If using dried cranberries, dried cherries, or raisins, soak them in water for 10 minutes to plump, then drain well.

Per serving: calories: 88, protein: 1 g, fat: 8 g, carbohydrate: 3 g, fiber: 1 g, sodium: 67 mg

Slightly sweet, crunchy, and aromatic, fennel frequently replaces celery in Mediterranean dishes.

green salad with fennel and cherry tomatoes

YIELD: 1 SERVING

2 cups torn red leaf, green leaf, or romaine lettuce

¼ cup thinly sliced fennel (see note)

2 small red radishes, thinly sliced (optional)

1½ tablespoons Classic Vinaigrette (page 113)
  or Lemon-Herb Dressing (page 120)

6 cherry tomatoes, halved

EQUIPMENT

salad spinner

measuring cups

cutting board

chef's knife, 8-inch

serrated knife, 5-inch

mandoline (optional, for thinly slicing fennel)

measuring spoons

medium bowl

tongs

serving plate

Put the lettuce, fennel, optional radishes, and vinaigrette in a medium bowl and toss gently. Transfer to a serving plate. Top with the cherry tomatoes. Serve immediately.

NOTE: To thinly slice a bulb of fennel, trim off the stems and a little of the hard base and cut the bulb in half lengthwise. Put each half cut-side down on the cutting board and thinly slice it crosswise with a sharp knife. For ultrathin and uniform slices, use a mandoline.

GREEN SALAD WITH FENNEL, CHERRY TOMATOES, AND WATERMELON: Omit the optional radishes. Add ½ cup of watermelon chunks along with the lettuce, fennel, and vinaigrette.

Per serving: calories: 138, protein: 1 g, fat: 13 g, carbohydrate: 5 g, fiber: 2 g, sodium: 109 mg

Nutrition-packed, this salad can be simple or deluxe, depending on how many ingredients you want.

garden salad

YIELD: 1 SERVING

BASIC SALAD

2 cups torn romaine or red leaf lettuce

1 cup baby spinach, lightly packed

¼ cucumber, peeled and thinly sliced

¼ carrot, peeled and shredded or thinly sliced

OPTIONAL INGREDIENTS

½ cup thinly sliced red cabbage

½ cup alfalfa or clover sprouts

½ avocado, chopped

¼ cup thinly sliced celery

¼ cup dulse leaves, or 2 tablespoons dulse flakes

¼ cup thinly sliced red or green onion

2 small radishes, sliced

2 cherry tomatoes, halved

DRESSING

2 tablespoons Lemon-Herb Dressing (page 120), **Tahini-Lemon Dressing** (page 123), **or other dressing of your choice** (see pages 113 to 122)

EQUIPMENT

salad spinner

measuring cups

cutting board

peeler

chef's knife, 8-inch

grater, or food processor fitted with a shredding disk

mandoline (optional)

measuring spoons

large bowl

tongs

Combine the lettuce, spinach, cucumber, and carrot in a large bowl with as many optional ingredients as you like. Add the dressing and toss until evenly distributed. Serve immediately.

Per serving: calories: 222, protein: 4 g, fat: 19 g, carbohydrate: 9 g, fiber: 5 g, sodium: 203 mg

My version looks like the traditional Caesar but replaces the egg yolk and anchovies with a delicious vegan Ranch Dressing (page 122).

caesar salad

½ head romaine lettuce, wilted outer leaves removed

3 tablespoons Ranch Dressing (page 122)

½ Roma tomato, seeded and diced

2 tablespoons thinly sliced black olives

6 very thin slices red onion (optional)

Freshly ground pepper (optional)

EQUIPMENT

cutting board

chef's knife, 8-inch

salad spinner

measuring spoons

medium bowl

tongs

serving plate

serrated knife, 5-inch

mandoline (optional, for thinly slicing onion)

Slice the lettuce into 1-inch strips. Wash and dry the strips using a salad spinner. Put the lettuce and the dressing in a medium bowl and toss to combine. Transfer to a serving plate and top with the tomato, olives, and optional onion and pepper. Serve immediately.

Per serving: calories: 199, protein: 6 g, fat: 16 g, carbohydrate: 10 g, fiber: 3 g, sodium: 286 mg

Vegetables in a variety of colors provide a broad range of nutrients. All the colors of the rainbow come together in this salad, making it beautiful as well as good for you.

rainbow salad

3 cups torn red leaf, green leaf, or romaine lettuce

¼ cup **Classic Vinaigrette** (page 113) **or Sweet Mustard Dressing** (page 121)

½ **cucumber, unpeeled, seeded, cut in half lengthwise, and thinly sliced into half-moons**

⅓ **cup peeled and shredded carrot**

2 **stalks celery, or 1 tomato, thinly sliced**

½ **small beet, peeled and shredded** (see note), **or** ½ **cup thinly sliced red cabbage**

¼ **cup thinly sliced radishes** (optional)

½ **yellow bell pepper, cut into thin strips** (optional)

EQUIPMENT

salad spinner

measuring cups

medium bowl

spoon

peeler

tongs

serving plates, two

cutting board

spoon

chef's knife, 8-inch

serrated knife, 5-inch

grater, or food processor fitted with a shredding disk

Put the lettuce and 1 tablespoon of the vinaigrette in a medium bowl and toss gently. Divide between two serving plates. On top of the lettuce on each plate, arrange separate mounds of the cucumber, carrot, celery, beet, and optional radishes and bell pepper. Drizzle with the remaining vinaigrette. Serve immediately.

NOTE: To peel a beet, slice off the top and bottom, then remove the peel with a sharp vegetable peeler, such as Oxo brand. Shred the beet with a grater or a food processor fitted with a shredding disk.

Per serving: calories: 292, protein: 7 g, fat: 17 g, carbohydrate: 28 g, fiber: 6 mg, sodium: 184 mg

In this satisfying salad, several vegetables are chopped into uniform pieces so you can taste all of them with each bite.

chopped salad

YIELD: 2 SERVINGS

2 cups chopped romaine lettuce

2 tomatoes, chopped

1 red, yellow, or orange bell pepper, chopped

½ cucumber, peeled, seeded, and chopped

2 tablespoons Classic Vinaigrette (page 113) or Lemon-Herb Dressing (page 120)

1 avocado, chopped

EQUIPMENT

salad spinner

cutting board

chef's knife, 8-inch

measuring cups

peeler

spoon

measuring spoons

medium bowl

rubber spatula

Put the lettuce, tomatoes, bell pepper, cucumber, and vinaigrette in a medium bowl and toss to combine. Add the avocado and toss gently. Serve immediately.

Per serving: calories: 273, protein: 4 g, fat: 22 g, carbohydrate: 11 g, fiber: 9 g, sodium: 80 mg

This is one of my lunch staples—so simple and easy, yet satisfying. The avocado becomes creamy enough to eliminate the need for additional dressing.

lettuce, tomato, and avocado salad

YIELD: 1 SERVING

3 cups mesclun or torn leaf lettuce

1 Roma tomato, chopped

½ avocado, chopped

1½ teaspoons freshly squeezed lemon or lime juice

Dash salt

EQUIPMENT

salad spinner

measuring cups

cutting board

chef's knife, 8-inch

citrus juicer or reamer

measuring spoons

medium bowl

Put all the ingredients in a medium bowl. Toss with your hands, very gently massaging the avocado into the lettuce. Serve immediately.

Per serving: calories: 197, protein: 5 g, fat: 14 g, carbohydrate: 9 g, fiber: 10 g, sodium: 171 mg

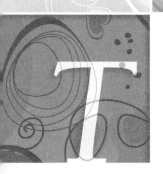

This retro dish is actually easier to make than tossed salads. To eat, cut the romaine lettuce into pieces with a knife and fork and mix with the dressing.

the wedge

YIELD: 1 SERVING

¼ head romaine lettuce

3 tablespoons Ranch Dressing (page 122).

EQUIPMENT

cutting board

chef's knife, 8-inch

measuring spoons

serving plate

Remove and discard the wilted outer leaves of the lettuce, and cut off about ½ inch of the top and bottom of the inner leaves. Wash the inner leaves and blot dry with paper towels.

Put the lettuce on a plate and pile the leaves into a wedge shape, fanning them out slightly. Top with the Ranch Dressing. Serve immediately.

Per serving: calories: 168, protein: 6 g, fat: 13 g, carbohydrate: 9 g, fiber: 2 g, sodium: 160 mg

The salsa and guacamole combine to make a rich dressing. No oil is needed.

taco salad

3 cups chopped romaine lettuce

⅓ cup fresh corn kernels (optional; see note)

¼ cup seeded and diced cucumbers (optional)

¼ cup Guacamole (page 67)

3 tablespoons salsa (preferably homemade, page 76)

EQUIPMENT

salad spinner

cutting board

chef's knife, 8-inch

measuring cups

spoon

measuring spoons

medium bowl

rubber spatula

Put all the ingredients in a medium bowl and toss to combine. Serve immediately.

NOTE: To remove the kernels from an ear of corn, stand the ear upright on a cutting board and slice the kernels off all sides with a sharp knife. One ear of corn yields about ⅓ cup of kernels.

Per serving: calories: 192, protein: 4 g, fat: 14 g, carbohydrate: 7 g, fiber: 10 g, sodium: 131 mg

A composed salad provides an elegant presentation, since ingredients are positioned carefully on the plate rather than randomly tossed. In this version, pear slices are fanned out, with dressed greens mounded on top.

composed salad with pears

YIELD: 1 SERVING

½ pear, thinly sliced

1½ tablespoons Classic Vinaigrette (page 113) or Apple Vinaigrette (page 113)

2 cups mesclun

EQUIPMENT

cutting board

chef's knife, 8-inch

serving plate

measuring spoons

salad spinner

measuring cups

small bowl

tongs

Fan the pear slices out on a serving plate and drizzle with about 1 teaspoon of the vinaigrette. Put the mesclun and the remaining vinaigrette in a small bowl and toss to combine. Mound on top of the pear. Serve immediately.

COMPOSED SALAD WITH PEACHES OR NECTARINES: Replace the pear with ½ peach or nectarine, thinly sliced.

Per serving: calories: 172, protein: 2 g, fat: 13 g, carbohydrate: 12 g, fiber: 3 g, sodium: 89 mg

Tart grapefruit complements creamy avocado and peppery arugula.

grapefruit and avocado salad

YIELD: 1 SERVING

1 grapefruit

2 cups torn red leaf lettuce

1 cup arugula

1 tablespoon Lemon-Herb Dressing (page 120),
   plus extra for drizzling

¼ avocado, thinly sliced

EQUIPMENT

cutting board

serrated knife, 5-inch

salad spinner

measuring cups

medium bowl

measuring spoons

tongs

serving plate

chef's knife, 8-inch

Using a 5-inch serrated knife, cut off the top and bottom of the grapefruit and remove the peel and white pith. Use the knife to separate the grapefruit into segments. Put the lettuce and arugula in a medium bowl. Add the dressing and toss gently. Transfer to a serving plate and arrange the grapefruit and avocado on top. Drizzle with additional dressing. Serve immediately.

Per serving: calories: 219, protein: 4 g, fat: 16 g, carbohydrate: 13 g, fiber: 5 g, sodium: 108 mg

Turn a salad into a crunchy lunch by adding nuts and dried fruit.

trail mix salad

YIELD: 1 SERVING

2 cups mesclun or torn red leaf lettuce

2 tablespoons chopped almonds, cashews, or pecans

1 tablespoon dark or golden raisins or chopped dates

1 teaspoon extra-virgin olive oil

Dash balsamic or cider vinegar

Dash salt

EQUIPMENT

salad spinner

measuring cups

measuring spoons

cutting board

chef's knife, 8-inch

small bowl

tongs

Put all the ingredients in a small bowl and toss to combine. Serve immediately.

Per serving: calories: 190, protein: 6 g, fat: 14 g, carbohydrate: 13 g, fiber: 4 g, sodium: 139 mg

Enjoy this salad as a delicious first course before a Garden Wrap (page 133).

greek salad

YIELD: 1 SERVING

2 cups torn romaine lettuce

1 Roma tomato, cut into chunks

¼ cucumber, peeled, seeded, and cubed

¼ cup thinly sliced red onion

¼ red bell pepper, cut into chunks

2 tablespoons sliced kalamata olives

1½ tablespoons Lemon-Herb Dressing (page 120)

EQUIPMENT

salad spinner

measuring cups

cutting board

serrated knife, 5-inch

peeler

spoon

chef's knife, 8-inch

mandoline (optional, for thinly slicing onion)

measuring spoons

medium bowl

tongs

Put all the ingredients in a medium bowl and toss to combine. Serve immediately.

Per serving: calories: 228, protein: 4 g, fat: 17 g, carbohydrate: 13 g, fiber: 5 g, sodium: 251 mg

This sophisticated salad works as a side dish or a meal. Crunchy yet juicy, it's refreshing as well as nutritious.

thai salad

YIELD: 1 SERVING

1 cup thinly sliced green or red cabbage

¼ cup peeled and shredded carrot

¼ red bell pepper, cut lengthwise into thin strips

1 tablespoon freshly squeezed lime juice

1 teaspoon sesame oil or extra-virgin olive oil

⅛ teaspoon salt

1 cup chopped romaine lettuce

½ Granny Smith apple, peeled and cut into thin strips (see note)

2 tablespoons chopped cashews, unsoaked

2 tablespoons chopped fresh cilantro

2 tablespoons unsweetened shredded dried coconut

EQUIPMENT

cutting board

chef's knife, 8-inch

mandoline (optional, for thinly slicing cabbage)

measuring cups

peeler

grater

citrus juicer or reamer

measuring spoons

medium bowl

salad spinner

rubber spatula

Put the cabbage, carrot, bell pepper, lime juice, oil, and salt in a medium bowl and massage gently with your hands to soften. Add the lettuce, apple, cashews, cilantro, and coconut and toss to combine. Stored in a sealed container in the refrigerator, Thai Salad will keep for 24 hours.

NOTE: To cut the apple into thin strips, stack several slices and cut lengthwise into matchsticks. Repeat with the remaining slices.

THAI SALAD WITH MOCK PEANUT SAUCE: Omit the lime juice, oil, salt, apple, cashews, and coconut. Add ¼ cup of Mock Peanut Sauce (page 75).

Per serving: calories: 287, protein: 6 g, fat: 20 g, carbohydrate: 21 g, fiber: 7 g, sodium: 310 mg

A sweet beginning to a fall or winter meal.

harvest salad

YIELD: 1 SERVING

2 cups torn red leaf lettuce

¼ apple or pear, unpeeled and thinly sliced, or ¼ cup halved seedless grapes

1½ tablespoons Classic Vinaigrette (page 113) or Apple Vinaigrette (page 113)

1 tablespoon chopped pecans, unsoaked

1 tablespoon fresh raspberries, dried cherries, or dried cranberries (see note)

EQUIPMENT

salad spinner

measuring cups

cutting board

chef's knife, 8-inch

measuring spoons

medium bowl

tongs

serving plate

Put the lettuce, apple, and vinaigrette in a medium bowl and toss gently. Transfer to a serving plate and arrange the pecans and raspberries on top. Serve immediately.

NOTE: If using dried cherries or cranberries, soak them in water for 10 minutes to plump, then drain well.

Per serving: calories: 197, protein: 2 g, fat: 18 g, carbohydrate: 7 g, fiber: 4 g, sodium: 115 mg

In Asian cultures, salads have featured mineral-rich sea vegetables for centuries. Arame, a popular variety in Japan, has a mild semisweet flavor. You can eat it raw—just soak briefly first.

arame salad

YIELD: 2 CUPS, 2 SERVINGS

½ ounce arame, soaked in water for 5 minutes and drained

1 carrot, peeled and shredded

½ cucumber, peeled, seeded, and diced

1 green onion, thinly sliced

2 teaspoons freshly squeezed lemon juice

2 teaspoons tamari

1 teaspoon sesame oil

½ teaspoon minced fresh ginger

Dash cayenne

EQUIPMENT

medium bowl

fine-mesh strainer

cutting board

peeler

grater

spoon

chef's knife, 8-inch

citrus juicer or reamer

measuring spoons

rubber spatula

Put all the ingredients in a medium bowl and toss to combine. Serve immediately.

WAKAME SALAD: Replace the arame with ½ ounce wakame, soaked in water for 10 minutes, drained, and chopped.

Per serving: calories: 58, protein: 2 g, fat: 2 g, carbohydrate: 6 g, fiber: 2 g, sodium: 334 mg

This traditional dish is a staple of Middle Eastern restaurants. It goes well with Zucchini Hummus (page 70).

jerusalem salad

YIELD: 1 SERVING

½ cucumber, peeled, seeded, and diced

½ tomato, seeded and diced

1 tablespoon Lemon-Herb Dressing (page 120) or Tahini-Lemon Dressing (page 123)

1 tablespoon minced onion

1 tablespoon minced fresh parsley

EQUIPMENT

cutting board

peeler

spoon

chef's knife, 8-inch

measuring spoons

small bowl

rubber spatula

Put all the ingredients in a small bowl and toss to combine. Serve immediately.

Per serving: calories: 122, protein: 2 g, fat: 9 g, carbohydrate: 8 g, fiber: 2 g, sodium: 79 mg

When they are available, multicolored heirloom tomatoes make this simple salad especially beautiful.

caprese salad

YIELD: 1 SERVING

2 regular or heirloom tomatoes, thinly sliced

⅛ teaspoon salt

1 tablespoon minced fresh basil or oregano

1 teaspoon extra-virgin olive oil

EQUIPMENT

cutting board

chef's knife, 8-inch

serrated knife, 5-inch

measuring spoons

serving plate

Arrange the tomatoes on a serving plate. Sprinkle with the salt and basil. Drizzle with the oil. Serve immediately.

Per serving: calories: 92, protein: 2 g, fat: 5 g, carbohydrate: 9 g, fiber: 3 g, sodium: 299 mg

This crunchy, spicy salad can become addictive. Finely dice the vegetables into uniform pieces for the most pleasing texture.

indian carrot and cucumber salad

½ pound carrots, peeled and diced

1 tomato, seeded and diced

½ cucumber, peeled, seeded, and diced

¼ cup minced fresh cilantro, packed

1 tablespoon freshly squeezed lime juice

1½ teaspoons extra-virgin olive oil

¼ teaspoon minced jalapeño chile, or dash cayenne

⅛ teaspoon salt

EQUIPMENT

cutting board

peeler

chef's knife, 8-inch

spoon

measuring cups

citrus juicer or reamer

measuring spoons

medium bowl

rubber spatula

Put all the ingredients in a medium bowl and toss to combine. Stored in a sealed container in the refrigerator, Indian Carrot and Cucumber Salad will keep for 2 days.

Per serving: calories: 103, protein: 3 g, fat: 4 g, carbohydrate: 13 g, fiber: 4 g, sodium: 225 mg

Serve with Papaya-Lime Soup (page 88) for a tropical summer lunch.

mango and avocado salad

YIELD: 1 SERVING

1 mango, cubed

½ avocado, cubed

2 teaspoons minced red onion

1 teaspoon minced fresh cilantro

1 teaspoon freshly squeezed lime juice

¼ teaspoon minced jalapeño chile, or dash cayenne

1 cup mesclun or chopped romaine lettuce

1 tablespoon Lime-Herb Dressing (page 120)

Put the mango, avocado, onion, cilantro, lime juice, and chile in a small bowl and toss gently. Arrange the mesclun on a serving plate and drizzle with the dressing. Mound the mango mixture on top of the lettuce. Serve immediately.

EQUIPMENT

cutting board

chef's knife, 8-inch

measuring spoons

citrus juicer or reamer

small bowl

rubber spatula

salad spinner

measuring cups

serving plate

Per serving: calories: 372, protein: 3 g, fat: 23 g, carbohydrate: 35 g, fiber: 11 g, sodium: 83 mg

Marinating thinly sliced raw beets in Lemon-Herb Dressing (page 120) makes them tender and delicious; it also imparts a beautiful fuchsia color to the dressing.

shaved beet salad

SEE PHOTO ON BACK COVER.

YIELD: 1 SERVING

½ small beet, peeled (see note) **and sliced ultrathin using a mandoline or sharp knife**

1½ tablespoons Lemon-Herb Dressing (page 120)

1½ cups mesclun or arugula

1 tablespoon chopped walnuts or pecans, unsoaked (optional)

EQUIPMENT

cutting board

chef's knife, 8-inch

peeler

mandoline (optional, for thinly slicing beets)

small bowl

measuring spoons

rubber spatula

salad spinner

measuring cups

serving plate

tongs

Put the beet in a small bowl, add the dressing, and toss until evenly coated. Let marinate for 30 minutes at room temperature, or up to 12 hours in the refrigerator. Arrange the mesclun on a serving plate. Remove the beets from the dressing and put them on top of the greens along with the optional walnuts. Drizzle with the remaining dressing left from marinating the beets. Serve immediately.

NOTE: To peel a beet, slice off the top and bottom, then remove the peel with a sharp vegetable peeler, such as Oxo brand.

Per serving: calories: 147, protein: 1 g, fat: 14 g, carbohydrate: 4 g, fiber: 1 g, sodium: 139 mg

This elegant salad is worth the expense of the Belgian endive and raddichio, two gourmet greens that can be found in most supermarkets.

tricolor salad

YIELD: 1 SERVING

1½ cups baby spinach or arugula, lightly packed

¾ cup chopped Belgian endive

¾ cup chopped radicchio

1½ tablespoons Classic Vinaigrette (page 113)

1 tablespoon chopped walnuts, unsoaked

EQUIPMENT

salad spinner

measuring cups

cutting board

chef's knife, 8-inch

measuring spoons

medium bowl

tongs

serving plate

Put the spinach, belgian endive, radicchio, and vinaigrette in a medium bowl. Lightly massage the greens for about 1 minute with your hands to soften them. Transfer to a serving plate and top with the walnuts. Serve immediately.

Per serving: calories: 190, protein: 5 g, fat: 17 g, carbohydrate: 4 g, fiber: 5 g, sodium: 161 mg

SALAD DRESSINGS

Classic Vinaigrette (page 113), Apple Vinaigrette (page 113), and Lemon-Herb Dressing (page 120) are my standby dressings, because they highlight the delicate flavors of greens without overpowering them. Other recipes provide variety and are especially delicious if you like creamy textures. My version of Ranch Dressing (page 122) is so rich, you won't miss the mayonnaise and sour cream. If you're cutting back on fat, Mango and Red Bell Pepper Dressing (page 119) is fat-free, and Avocado-Lime Dressing (page 115) delivers flavor without oil.

For a simple dressing, drizzle extra-virgin olive oil on your salad, toss, add a little lemon or lime juice, and toss again. That's it! Other simple additions include a dash of salt and a small amount of crushed garlic. You can also use nut and seed oils, such as walnut or flaxseed oil, instead of olive oil. If you wish to avoid oil altogether, just go with the lemon or lime juice and salt. They make a fine dressing, especially if your salad contains avocado, which gets creamy when tossed.

Cider vinegar is easier to digest than red wine varieties, and it has a fine fruity flavor. For a more traditional taste, substitute balsamic vinegar.

classic vinaigrette

YIELD: ⅔ CUP, 6 SERVINGS

6 tablespoons extra-virgin olive oil

2 tablespoons cider or balsamic vinegar

2 tablespoons water

1 teaspoon Dijon mustard (optional)

¼ teaspoon salt

Dash ground pepper

EQUIPMENT

measuring spoons

blender

Put all the ingredients in a blender and process on medium speed until smooth and creamy. Stored in a sealed jar in the refrigerator, Classic Vinaigrette will keep for 1 week.

CLASSIC VINAIGRETTE WITH PARSLEY AND SHALLOTS: Add 1 teaspoon of minced fresh parsley and 1 teaspoon of minced shallots.

Per serving: calories: 122, protein: 0 g, fat: 14 g, carbohydrate: 0 g, fiber: 0 g, sodium: 111 mg

Apple juice makes this dressing delightfully mild, fruity, and light.

apple vinaigrette

YIELD: ½ CUP, 4 SERVINGS

3 tablespoons apple juice

1 tablespoon cider vinegar

¼ teaspoon salt

¼ teaspoon crushed garlic

Dash ground pepper (optional)

3 tablespoons extra-virgin olive oil

EQUIPMENT

measuring spoons

garlic press

small bowl

whisk

Put the apple juice, vinegar, salt, garlic, and optional pepper in a small bowl and whisk to combine. Add the oil and whisk until smooth. Stored in a sealed jar in the refrigerator, Apple Vinaigrette will keep for 3 days.

Per serving: calories: 97, protein: 0 g, fat: 10 g, carbohydrate: 2 g, fiber: 0 g, sodium: 134 mg

This perfectly balanced dressing is zesty, herbaceous, and slightly sweet.

creamy dill dressing

YIELD: 1 CUP, 8 SERVINGS

½ cup extra-virgin olive oil

2 tablespoons minced fresh dill

2 tablespoons cider vinegar

2 tablespoons water

1 tablespoon agave nectar or maple syrup

1 tablespoon freshly squeezed lime juice

¼ teaspoon salt, plus a pinch

EQUIPMENT

measuring cups

cutting board

chef's knife, 8-inch

measuring spoons

citrus juicer or reamer

blender

rubber spatula

Put all the ingredients in a blender and process on medium speed until smooth. Stored in a sealed jar in the refrigerator, Creamy Dill Dressing will keep for 3 days.

Per serving: calories: 128, protein: 0 g, fat: 14 g, carbohydrate: 2 g, fiber: 0 g, sodium: 75 mg

Can you skip the oil when you want a rich and creamy dressing? Absolutely! Just replace it with avocado, which is lower in calories and higher in fiber and other nutrients.

avocado-lime dressing

SEE PHOTO FACING PAGE 120.

YIELD: 1 CUP, 4 SERVINGS

½ **cup mashed avocado** (1 avocado)

½ **cup water**

1 **tablespoon minced fresh dill, basil, or mint**

1 **tablespoon freshly squeezed lime juice**

¼ **teaspoon salt**

EQUIPMENT

cutting board

chef's knife, 8-inch

small bowl

fork

measuring cups

measuring spoons

citrus juicer or reamer

blender

rubber spatula

Put all the ingredients in a blender and process on medium speed until smooth. Stored in a sealed jar in the refrigerator, Avocado-Lime Dressing will keep for 2 days.

Per serving: calories: 73, protein: 1 g, fat: 7 g, carbohydrate: 1 g, fiber: 3 g, sodium: 137 mg

Not much fat on this goddess—just a tablespoon of nuts per generous serving.

goddess dressing

YIELD: 1 CUP, 4 SERVINGS

½ cup water

¼ cup chopped fresh basil, packed

¼ cup soaked cashews (see page 7)

¼ cup freshly squeezed lemon juice

¼ cup chopped fresh parsley, packed

2 tablespoons chopped red or green onion

1 teaspoon agave nectar or maple syrup

¼ teaspoon salt

EQUIPMENT

measuring cups

cutting board

chef's knife, 8-inch

citrus juicer or reamer

measuring spoons

blender

rubber spatula

Put all the ingredients in a blender and process on medium speed until smooth. Stored in a sealed jar in the refrigerator, Goddess Dressing will keep for 3 days.

Per serving: calories: 65, protein: 2 g, fat: 4 g, carbohydrate: 6 g, fiber: 1 g, sodium: 137 mg

This sweet dressing is delectable with mesclun, spinach, or arugula.

fig dressing

YIELD: ¾ CUP, 6 SERVINGS

3 dried figs, trimmed, soaked in water for 10 minutes and drained

¼ cup extra-virgin olive oil

¼ cup water

1 tablespoon freshly squeezed lemon juice

1 tablespoon balsamic vinegar

¼ teaspoon salt

Dash ground pepper

EQUIPMENT

cutting board

paring knife

small bowl

small colander or fine-mesh strainer

measuring cups

citrus juicer or reamer

measuring spoons

blender

rubber spatula

Put all the ingredients in a blender and process on medium speed until smooth. Stored in a sealed jar in the refrigerator, Fig Dressing will keep for 3 days.

Per serving: calories: 107, protein: 0 g, fat: 9 g, carbohydrate: 6 g, fiber: 1 g, sodium: 91 mg

Cucumbers become creamy when blended, yet remain light and refreshing. Try the red bell pepper and tomato variations too.

creamy cucumber dressing

YIELD: 1 CUP, 8 SERVINGS

1 small cucumber, peeled, seeded, and chopped

¼ cup extra-virgin olive oil

1½ tablespoons freshly squeezed lemon juice

¼ teaspoon salt

¼ teaspoon crushed garlic

Dash cayenne (optional)

1½ teaspoons minced fresh dill or basil, or ½ teaspoon dried

1 teaspoon minced red or yellow onion

EQUIPMENT

cutting board

peeler

spoon

chef's knife, 8-inch

measuring cups

citrus juicer or reamer

measuring spoons

garlic press

blender

rubber spatula

Put the cucumber, oil, lemon juice, salt, garlic, and cayenne in a blender and process on medium speed until smooth and creamy. Add the dill and onion and process on medium speed briefly, just to mix. Stored in a sealed jar in the refrigerator, Creamy Cucumber Dressing will keep for 3 days.

CREAMY RED BELL PEPPER DRESSING: Replace the cucumber with 1 small red bell pepper, chopped.

CREAMY TOMATO DRESSING: Replace the cucumber with 2 tomatoes, chopped. Decrease the lemon juice to 1 tablespoon.

Per serving: calories: 126, protein: 0 g, fat: 14 g, carbohydrate: 2 g, fiber: 0 g, sodium: 68 mg

Magic—thick and luscious fat-free dressing with just two ingredients!

mango and red bell pepper dressing

SEE PHOTO FACING PAGE 120.

YIELD: 1 CUP, 4 SERVINGS

¾ cup chopped red bell pepper (½ red bell pepper)

¾ cup chopped fresh mango (1 mango)

2 teaspoons balsamic vinegar (optional)

EQUIPMENT

cutting board

chef's knife, 8-inch

measuring cups

measuring spoons

blender

rubber spatula

Put all the ingredients in a blender and process on high speed until smooth and creamy. Stored in a sealed jar in the refrigerator, Mango and Red Bell Pepper Dressing will keep for 24 hours.

Per serving: calories: 25, protein: 0 g, fat: 0 g, carbohydrate: 6 g, fiber: 1 g, sodium: 1 mg

Pesto (page 78) can become a salad dressing in seconds.

pesto dressing

YIELD: ½ CUP, 4 SERVINGS

½ cup Pesto (page 78)

2 tablespoons freshly squeezed lemon juice

EQUIPMENT

measuring cups

citrus juicer or reamer

measuring spoons

small bowl

spoon

Put the pesto and lemon juice in a small bowl and stir to combine. Stored in a sealed jar in the refrigerator, Pesto Dressing will keep for 5 days.

Per serving: calories: 131, protein: 2 g, fat: 14 g, carbohydrate: 2 g, fiber: 1 g, sodium: 70 mg

This dressing adds zing and fragrance to even the simplest green salad. Vary the taste with different fresh herbs.

lemon-herb dressing

YIELD: ¾ CUP, 8 SERVINGS

¼ **cup freshly squeezed lemon juice**

1 tablespoon minced fresh herbs (such as parsley, basil, dill, mint, tarragon, or oregano)

½ **teaspoon crushed garlic**

¼ **teaspoon plus** ⅛ **teaspoon salt**

¼ **teaspoon Dijon mustard** (optional)

Dash ground pepper (optional)

½ **cup extra-virgin olive oil**

EQUIPMENT

citrus juicer or reamer

measuring cups

cutting board

chef's knife, 8-inch

measuring spoons

garlic press

small bowl

whisk

Put the lemon juice, herbs, garlic, salt, and optional mustard and pepper in a small bowl and whisk to combine. Add the oil and whisk until well combined. Stored in a sealed jar in the refrigerator, Lemon-Herb Dressing will keep for 5 days.

CREAMY LEMON-HERB DRESSING: Put all the ingredients in a blender and process on medium speed until smooth and creamy.

LIME-HERB DRESSING: Replace the lemon juice with ¼ cup of freshly squeezed lime juice.

SPICY CILANTRO-LIME DRESSING: Replace the lemon juice with ¼ cup of freshly squeezed lime juice. Use 1 tablespoon of cilantro as the fresh herb. Add ⅛ teaspoon of cayenne and a dash of ground cumin.

Per serving: calories: 121, protein: 0 g, fat: 14 g, carbohydrate: 1 g, fiber: 0 g, sodium: 102 mg

Avocado-Lime Dressing, *page 115***, Mango and Red Bell Pepper Dressing,** *page 119,* **and Tahini-Lemon Dressing,** *page 123*

Crudités, *page 91,* **and Mock Sour Cream and Chive Dip,** *page 68*

Garden Wrap, *page 133*

Not Tuna Rolls, *page 134*

This sweet-and-tangy dressing keeps your veggies interesting.

sweet mustard dressing

YIELD: ¾ CUP, 8 SERVINGS

½ cup extra-virgin olive oil

¼ cup cider vinegar or freshly squeezed lemon juice

1 tablespoon Dijon mustard

2 teaspoons maple syrup or agave nectar

½ teaspoon crushed garlic

¼ teaspoon plus ⅛ teaspoon salt

Dash ground pepper

EQUIPMENT

measuring cups

measuring spoons

garlic press

blender

rubber spatula

Put all the ingredients in a blender and process on medium speed until smooth and creamy. Stored in a sealed jar in the refrigerator, Sweet Mustard Dressing will keep for 1 week.

Per serving: calories: 128, protein: 0 g, fat: 14 g, carbohydrate: 1 g, fiber: 0 g, sodium: 151 mg

This dressing tastes so rich and creamy, you won't believe it's dairy-free.

ranch dressing

SEE PHOTO FACING PAGE 88. **YIELD: 1 CUP, 8 SERVINGS**

1 cup soaked cashews (see page 7)

¾ cup water

2 tablespoons freshly squeezed lemon juice

½ teaspoon garlic powder

½ teaspoon onion powder

¼ teaspoon plus ⅛ teaspoon salt

1 tablespoon minced fresh basil, or 1 teaspoon dried

1 tablespoon minced fresh dill, or 1 teaspoon dried dill weed

EQUIPMENT

measuring cups

citrus juicer or reamer

measuring spoons

cutting board

chef's knife, 8-inch

blender

rubber spatula

Put the cashews, water, lemon juice, garlic powder, onion powder, and salt in a blender and process on high speed until smooth and creamy. Add the basil and dill and pulse briefly, just to mix. Stored in a sealed jar in the refrigerator, Ranch Dressing will keep for 5 days.

THOUSAND ISLAND DRESSING: Add ½ red bell pepper, chopped, to the blender along with the cashews.

Per serving: calories: 106, protein: 3 g, fat: 8 g, carbohydrate: 5 g, fiber: 1 g, sodium: 104 mg

This dressing adds Middle Eastern flavor to Garden Salad (page 94) or Rainbow Salad (page 96).

tahini-lemon dressing

SEE PHOTO FACING PAGE 120.   YIELD: 1 CUP, 8 SERVINGS

½ cup raw tahini

⅓ cup water

¼ cup freshly squeezed lemon juice

½ teaspoon crushed garlic

¼ teaspoon ground cumin

¼ teaspoon salt

Dash cayenne

1 tablespoon minced fresh parsley

EQUIPMENT

measuring cups

citrus juicer or reamer

garlic press

measuring spoons

blender

rubber spatula

Put the tahini, water, lemon juice, garlic, cumin, salt, and cayenne in a blender and process on medium speed until smooth. Add the parsley and pulse briefly, just to mix. Stored in a sealed jar in the refrigerator, Tahini-Lemon Dressing will keep for 2 days.

Per serving: calories: 88, protein: 3 g, fat: 7 g, carbohydrate: 3 g, fiber: 1 g, sodium: 78 mg

SANDWICHES

A sandwich is convenient at lunch because it's portable and fills you up. But with two pieces of bread, a typical sandwich is a high-carb, high-gluten meal that can leave you feeling tired and sluggish. I suggest replacing the bread with romaine lettuce. Just spread one lettuce leaf with leftover pâté, dip, or avocado, add some sprouts and tomato slices, and put another lettuce leaf on top. Then eat it with your hands, just like a traditional sandwich!

Move over, mayonnaise—guacamole is heavenly on a sandwich.

guacamole sandwich

YIELD: 1 SERVING

2 large leaves romaine
  lettuce

¼ cup Guacamole (page 67)

½ Roma tomato, sliced

EQUIPMENT

measuring cups

rubber spatula

cutting board

serrated knife, 5-inch

Spread one of the lettuce leaves with the guacamole and arrange the tomato over it. Put the second lettuce leaf on top. Serve immediately.

Per serving: calories: 164, protein: 3 g, fat: 14 g, carbohydrate: 5 g, fiber: 7 g, sodium: 15 mg

This tuna-friendly sandwich makes a comforting lunch.

not tuna sandwich

YIELD: 1 SERVING

2 large leaves romaine
  lettuce

⅓ cup Not Tuna Pâté
  (page 71)

½ cup alfalfa or clover
  sprouts

6 thin slices peeled
  cucumber

1 Roma tomato, sliced

EQUIPMENT

measuring cups

rubber spatula

cutting board

peeler

serrated knife, 5-inch

chef's knife, 8-inch

Spread one of the lettuce leaves with the pâté and arrange the sprouts, cucumber, and tomato over it. Put the second lettuce leaf on top. Serve immediately.

Per serving: calories: 198, protein: 8 g, fat: 15 g, carbohydrate: 10 g, fiber: 5 g, sodium: 239 mg

Skip the pita bread and fried falafel for a delicious, lighter version of this Middle Eastern favorite.

hummus sandwich

SEE PHOTO FACING PAGE 57.

YIELD: 1 SERVING

2 large leaves romaine lettuce

⅓ cup **Zucchini Hummus** (page 70)

¼ red bell pepper, sliced into rings

2 tablespoons sliced black olives

EQUIPMENT

measuring cups

rubber spatula

cutting board

serrated knife, 5-inch

chef's knife, 8-inch

Spread one of the lettuce leaves with the hummus and arrange the bell pepper and olives over it. Put the second lettuce leaf on top. Serve immediately.

HUMMUS SANDWICH WITH MUSTARD: Spread one of the lettuce leaves with ½ teaspoon of Dijon mustard before spreading with the hummus. Replace the bell pepper and olives with ½ cup of mesclun and 2 tomato slices. Put the second lettuce leaf on top. Serve immediately.

Per serving: calories: 113, protein: 3 g, fat: 8 g, carbohydrate: 6 g, fiber: 3 g, sodium: 320 mg

This hearty sandwich will stick to your ribs all afternoon.

walnut pâté sandwich

YIELD: 1 SERVING

2 large leaves romaine lettuce

⅓ cup Walnut Pâté (page 72) **or Pecan Pâté** (page 72)

½ cup alfalfa or clover sprouts

6 thin slices peeled cucumber

¼ cup peeled and shredded carrot (optional)

1 Roma tomato, sliced

1 tablespoon Sweet Mustard Dressing
(page 121; optional)

EQUIPMENT

measuring cups

rubber spatula

cutting board

peeler

serrated knife, 5-inch

measuring spoons

Spread one of the lettuce leaves with the pâté and arrange the sprouts, cucumber, optional carrot, and tomato over it. Drizzle with the dressing if desired. Put the second lettuce leaf on top. Serve immediately.

Per serving: calories: 299, protein: 8 g, fat: 27 g, carbohydrate: 7 g, fiber: 5 g, sodium: 184 mg

Enjoy the familiar flavors of pizza, without the heaviness of bread and cheese.

pizza sandwich

YIELD: 1 SERVING

2 large leaves romaine lettuce

⅓ cup Marinara Sauce (page 74)

½ Roma tomato, sliced

¼ avocado, sliced

6 thin slices onion

1 cremini mushroom, thinly sliced

2 tablespoons chopped black olives

Dash salt

EQUIPMENT

measuring cups

rubber spatula

cutting board

serrated knife, 5-inch

chef's knife, 8-inch

measuring spoons

Spread one of the lettuce leaves with the sauce and arrange the tomato, avocado, onion, mushroom, and olives over it. Sprinkle with salt. Put the second lettuce leaf on top. Serve immediately.

PIZZA SALAD: Replace the lettuce leaves with 3 cups of chopped romaine lettuce and toss with the sauce, tomato, avocado, onion, mushroom, olives, and salt.

Per serving: calories: 214, protein: 4 g, fat: 15 g, carbohydrate: 13 g, fiber: 7 g, sodium: 333 mg

Lay the veggie filling on thick—this sub is packed with flavor, not calories.

veggie sub

YIELD: 1 SERVING

2 large leaves romaine lettuce

½ cup alfalfa or clover sprouts

¼ avocado, sliced

6 thin slices peeled cucumber

½ Roma tomato, sliced

6 thin slices onion

1 tablespoon Ranch Dressing (page 122)

EQUIPMENT

measuring cups

cutting board

peeler

chef's knife, 8-inch

serrated knife, 5-inch

mandoline (optional, for thinly slicing cucumber and onion)

measuring spoons

Arrange the sprouts, avocado, cucumber, tomato, and onion on one leaf of the romaine lettuce. Drizzle with the dressing. Put the second lettuce leaf on top. Serve immediately.

Per serving: calories: 161, protein: 5 g, fat: 11 g, carbohydrate: 8 g, fiber: 6 g, sodium: 66 mg

Not so sloppy—but oh so satisfying.

sloppy joe

YIELD: 1 SERVING

2 large leaves romaine lettuce

¼ cup **Walnut Pâté** (page 72) **or Pecan Pâté** (page 72)

¼ cup **Marinara Sauce** (page 74)

6 thin slices peeled cucumber

6 thin slices onion

¼ cup peeled and shredded carrot (optional)

½ **Roma tomato, sliced**

EQUIPMENT

measuring cups

rubber spatula

cutting board

peeler

chef's knife, 8-inch

serrated knife, 5-inch

mandoline (optional, for thinly slicing cucumber and onion)

grater (optional)

Spread one of the lettuce leaves with the pâté, then the sauce. Arrange the cucumber, onion, optional carrot, and tomato over it. Put the second lettuce leaf on top. Serve immediately.

Per serving: calories: 307, protein: 8 g, fat: 25 g, carbohydrate: 13 g, fiber: 6 g, sodium: 295 mg

Apple slices replace bread in this crunchy twist on the peanut butter sandwich.

apple sandwiches

SEE PHOTO FACING PAGE 25.

YIELD: 2 SANDWICHES, 1 SERVING

1 apple, unpeeled

2 tablespoons raw almond or cashew butter
(preferably homemade, page 78)

2 teaspoons raisins (optional)

EQUIPMENT

cutting board

chef's knife, 8-inch

paring knife

measuring spoons

Slice the apple thinly crosswise and remove the seeds and core with a paring knife. Spread 1 apple slice with 1 tablespoon of the almond butter and top with 1 teaspoon of the raisins if desired. Put another apple slice on top. Repeat with 2 additional apple slices. Serve immediately.

APPLE-BANANA SANDWICHES: Omit the raisins. For each sandwich, arrange a few thin slices of banana on top of the almond butter.

JAM AND APPLE SANDWICHES: Omit the raisins. For each sandwich, spread 1 tablespoon of Raspberry Jam (page 34) on top of the almond butter.

NOT TUNA AND APPLE SANDWICHES: Omit the almond butter. Fill each sandwich with 3 tablespoons of Not Tuna Pâté (page 71) and the optional raisins.

Per serving: calories: 194, protein: 5 g, fat: 12 g, carbohydrate: 18 g, fiber: 5 g, sodium: 23 mg

ENTRÉES

No matter how delicious a raw soup or salad is, you may desire a main dish as well. You don't have to spend hours making dehydrated mock pizzas or mock burgers. With a few greens or vegetables and some leftover pâté or dip, you can use the techniques of stacking, stuffing, and rolling to create an elegant dish in a snap. Stacking transforms tomatoes and Pesto (page 78) into a Tomato Stack (page 140). If you have Not Tuna Pâté (page 71) or Guacamole (page 67) on hand, you can make a Stuffed Bell Pepper (page 142), Stuffed Tomato (page 142), or Stuffed Mushroom (page 138) in five minutes. California Rolls (page 134) are the classic rolled entrée, but a Garden Wrap (page 133) or Spring Roll (page 137) is also satisfying. Raw entrées can be served either alone or with a vegetable side dish (see pages 144 to 153).

Ditch the tortillas and grab some collards—this veggie-filled wrap is full of flavor.

garden wrap

SEE PHOTO FACING PAGE 121.

YIELD: 1 SERVING

½ cup thinly sliced mushrooms

6 thin slices onion

2 teaspoons tamari

1 medium leaf collard greens

¼ avocado, sliced

¼ cucumber, peeled, seeded, and cut lengthwise into thin strips

¼ cup peeled and shredded carrot or carrot ribbons (see Tools and Techniques, page 11)

EQUIPMENT

cutting board

chef's knife, 8-inch

measuring cups

mandoline (optional, for thinly slicing onion)

measuring spoons

medium bowl

rubber spatula

peeler

spoon

grater

Put the mushrooms, onion, and tamari in a medium bowl and toss to combine. Work the tamari into the vegetables using a rubber spatula or your hands. Let marinate for 10 minutes. Drain off any excess tamari. Cut off the thickest part of the collard leaf stem. Lay the collard leaf horizontally on the cutting board, with the stem parallel to you and the underside facing up. Layer the mushrooms, onions, avocado, cucumber, and carrot on the leaf. Roll up the leaf burrito-style, tucking in the ends as you go. Slice the roll into 2 pieces. Serve immediately.

Per serving: calories: 122, protein: 4 g, fat: 7 g, carbohydrate: 8 g, fiber: 5 g, sodium: 324 mg

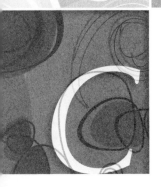

With a little practice, you'll be rolling sushi like a pro. California Rolls make stunning appetizers at any party and satisfying sandwich substitutes for lunch.

california rolls

2 sheets nori

2 teaspoons mellow white miso

2 cups alfalfa or clover sprouts (optional)

¼ cucumber, peeled, seeded, and cut lengthwise into thin strips

½ avocado, thinly sliced

¼ cup peeled and shredded carrot or carrot ribbons (see Tools and Techniques, page 11)

¼ red bell pepper, cut lengthwise into thin strips

Tamari for dipping (optional)

EQUIPMENT

bamboo sushi mat

measuring spoons

measuring cups

cutting board

peeler

spoon

chef's knife, 8-inch

grater

small bowl with water, for sealing the roll

serrated knife, 5-inch

plate

small bowl for serving tamari (optional)

Lay one sheet of the nori, shiny-side down, on a bamboo sushi mat. Using the back of a teaspoon, spread 1 teaspoon of the miso in a single horizontal strip anywhere along the bottom third of the nori. Along the edge of the nori closest to you, layer half of the optional sprouts, cucumber, avocado, carrot, and bell pepper. To roll, grip the edges of the nori sheet and the sushi mat together with your thumbs and forefingers and press the filling back toward you with your other fingers. Using the mat to help you, roll the front edge of the nori over the filling. Squeeze it with the mat, then lift the mat and continue rolling. Just before completing the roll, dip your index finger in water and run it along the far edge of the nori sheet. This will seal the seam of the roll. Cut the roll into 6 pieces with a serrated knife. Fill, roll, and slice the other sheet of nori the same way. Arrange on a plate. Serve immediately, with a small bowl of tamari for dipping if desired.

NOT TUNA ROLLS: Replace the avocado with ¼ cup of Not Tuna Pâté, using 2 tablespoons per roll.

SEE PHOTO FACING PAGE 121.

Per serving: calories: 108, protein: 3 g, fat: 7 g, carbohydrate: 6 g, fiber: 5 g, sodium: 150 mg

This wheat-free lasagne has an authentic Italian flavor. Strips of zucchini replace the noodles, and avocado replaces the cheese.

lasagne

YIELD: 2 SERVINGS

½ **zucchini, unpeeled**

2 cups spinach leaves, firmly packed

½ **cup Marinara Sauce** (page 74)

½ **avocado, mashed**

EQUIPMENT

mandoline (optional, for slicing zucchini)

cutting board

chef's knife, 8-inch

measuring cups

food processor

rubber spatula

small bowl

fork

6-inch square glass container (such as a container used for leftovers)

measuring spoons

Thinly slice the zucchini lengthwise into long, wide noodles using a mandoline or a sharp knife. Put the spinach in a food processor fitted with the S blade and pulse or process until finely chopped. Transfer to a small bowl.

Coat the bottom of a 6-inch square glass container with 2 tablespoons of the sauce. Layer one-third of the zucchini noodles over the sauce. Top with 2 more tablespoons of the sauce. Layer half of the avocado over the sauce. Top with half of the spinach and press with a rubber spatula. Repeat this layering process one more time, starting with a layer of the zucchini. One-third of the zucchini and 2 tablespoons of the sauce will remain. Layer the remaining zucchini on top and cover with the sauce. Stored in a sealed container in the refrigerator, Lasagne will keep for 2 days.

Per serving: calories: 159, protein: 5 g, fat: 11 g, carbohydrate: 9 g, fiber: 7 g, sodium: 204 mg

Avocado halves are nature's perfect container for juicy salsa.

avocado boat

YIELD: 1 SERVING

½ **avocado, peeled and pitted** (see page 11)

¼ **cup Salsa** (page 76) **or Mango Salsa** (page 77)

EQUIPMENT

cutting board

chef's knife, 8-inch

teaspoon

measuring cups

Use a teaspoon to remove a small amount of the avocado flesh to create a cavity. Fill with the salsa. Serve immediately.

Per serving: calories: 172, protein: 3 g, fat: 14 g, carbohydrate: 6 g, fiber: 7 g, sodium: 157 mg

Serve alone or with Zucchini Pasta with Marinara (page 139) for an Italian dinner.

not meatballs

SEE PHOTO FACING PAGE 89.

YIELD: 1 SERVING

⅓ **cup Walnut Pâté** (page 72)

3 **tablespoons Marinara Sauce** (page 74)

EQUIPMENT

measuring cups

serving plate

measuring spoons

Form the pâté into 2 or 3 balls and put on a serving plate. Cover each ball with a thin coating of the sauce. Serve immediately.

PESTO NOT MEATBALLS: Replace the Marinara Sauce with 3 tablespoons of Pesto (page 78).

Per serving: calories: 331, protein: 8 g, fat: 31 g, carbohydrate: 8 g, fiber: 4 g, sodium: 294 mg

Spring rolls make a delicious centerpiece for any Asian-themed meal. For a more traditional roll, replace the cabbage leaf with rice paper that has been softened in water. Serve with Miso Soup (page 86) or Ramen (page 87).

spring roll

1 leaf Savoy or napa cabbage

½ cup mung bean sprouts or chopped green leaf lettuce

¼ cup peeled and shredded carrot or carrot ribbons (see Tools and Techniques, page 11)

¼ cucumber, peeled and made into ribbons (see Tools and Techniques, page 11)

2 sprigs cilantro, or 2 leaves mint

1½ tablespoons Mock Peanut Sauce (page 75), plus extra for dipping

EQUIPMENT

cutting board

chef's knife, 8-inch

measuring cups

peeler

grater

measuring spoons

Cut off the thickest part of the cabbage leaf stem. Lay the leaf horizontally on the cutting board, with the stem parallel to you and the underside facing up. Layer the sprouts, carrot, cucumber, and cilantro on the leaf. Drizzle with the sauce. Roll up the leaf burrito-style, tucking in the ends as you go. Slice the roll into 2 pieces. Serve immediately.

VEGETABLES WITH MOCK PEANUT SAUCE: Omit the cabbage leaf. Toss the sprouts, carrot, cucumber, and cilantro with the sauce. Serve immediately.

Per serving: calories: 83, protein: 4 g, fat: 3 g, carbohydrate: 10 g, fiber: 4 g, sodium: 90 mg

The sun-dried tomatoes in the pâté stuffing provide intense color and flavor in this appetizing dish.

stuffed mushroom

SEE PHOTO BETWEEN PAGES 152 AND 153.

YIELD: 1 SERVING

1 portobello mushroom, stemmed

1½ teaspoons tamari

¼ cup Sunflower Seed and Sun-Dried Tomato Pâté
(page 73)

½ teaspoon minced fresh parsley, for garnish

EQUIPMENT

cutting board

chef's knife, 8-inch

teaspoon

small bowl

measuring spoons

plate

measuring cup

rubber spatula

Use a teaspoon to remove enough of the inside of the mushroom cap to create a cavity for stuffing. Put the cap in a small bowl, sprinkle with the tamari, and turn several times until the cap is evenly coated. Let marinate for 5 to 30 minutes. Blot dry with a paper towel to remove any excess tamari. Put the mushroom cap on a plate, with the inside of the cap facing up. Stuff with the pâté and garnish with the parsley. Serve immediately.

STUFFED MUSHROOM APPETIZERS: Replace the portobello mushroom with 8 cremini or button mushrooms and use an additional ½ teaspoon of tamari. Stuff each with 1½ teaspoons of pâté. Yield: 4 servings.

Per serving: calories: 192, protein: 8 g, fat: 15 g, carbohydrate: 9 g, fiber: 3 g, sodium: 579 mg

You won't miss wheat pasta in this flavorful Italian entrée. For an elegant presentation, serve in a shallow bowl atop sliced tomatoes.

zucchini pasta al pesto

YIELD: 1 SERVING

2 zucchini, peeled
3 tablespoons Pesto (page 78)
4 thin tomato slices, for serving (optional)

EQUIPMENT
peeler
vegetable spiral slicer
cutting board
chef's knife, 8-inch
medium bowl
measuring spoons
tongs
shallow serving bowl

Cut the zucchini into thin noodles using a vegetable spiral slicer. Alternatively, use a vegetable peeler to create long ribbons, or "fettuccine," by drawing the peeler down all sides of the zucchini until you reach the core. Put in a medium bowl and toss with the pesto. Serve immediately in a shallow bowl on top of the sliced tomatoes if desired.

WARMING OPTION: Put the pesto in a small saucepan over low heat and warm for about 1 minute, taking care not to overheat it. Toss with the pasta. Serve immediately.

THAI ZUCCHINI NOODLES: Omit the optional tomato slices. Replace the Pesto with ¼ cup of Mock Peanut Sauce (page 75).

ZUCCHINI FETTUCCINE ALFREDO: Toss the zucchini noodles with ¼ cup of Ranch Dressing (page 122). Serve on top of the sliced tomatoes if desired.

ZUCCHINI PASTA WITH MARINARA OR PUTTANESCA SAUCE: Omit the optional tomato slices. Replace the Pesto with ⅓ cup of Marinara Sauce (page 74) or Puttanesca Sauce (page 74).

SEE PHOTO FACING PAGE 89.

Per serving: calories: 208, protein: 6 g, fat: 16 g, carbohydrate: 10 g, fiber: 5 g, sodium: 192 mg

This traditional *tapas* (Spanish hors d'oeuvre) usually includes bacon, sausage, and cheese, but you won't miss a thing in these savory-sweet raw bites. Serve them as an appetizer or a main course.

stuffed dates in marinara sauce

YIELD: 2 SERVINGS

8 pitted medjool dates, unsoaked

3 tablespoons Walnut Pâté (page 72)

⅔ cup Marinara Sauce or Middle Eastern Marinara Sauce (page 74)

EQUIPMENT

measuring spoons

measuring cups

small saucepan

wooden spoon

Stuff each date with about 1 teaspoon of pâté. Press the date halves back together around the pâté. Put the sauce and the stuffed dates in a small saucepan. Warm for 2 to 3 minutes over low heat, stirring gently, until the sauce is warm to the touch. Serve immediately.

Per serving: calories: 250, protein: 4 g, fat: 13 g, carbohydrate: 29 g, fiber: 6 g, sodium: 246 mg

Juicy tomatoes complement a rich pâté or pesto perfectly. Serve with a knife and fork for easy eating.

tomato stack

SEE PHOTO FACING PAGE 152.

YIELD: 1 SERVING

2 large slices tomato

¼ cup Not Tuna Pâté (page 71), Walnut Pâté (page 72), **or** Pesto (page 78)

2 tablespoons alfalfa or clover sprouts

1 teaspoon sliced black olives

EQUIPMENT

cutting board

serrated knife, 5-inch

plate

measuring cups

measuring spoons

Put 1 tomato slice on a plate and spread 2 tablespoons of the pâté over it. Cover with the second tomato slice and spread with the remaining 2 tablespoons of pâté. Top with the sprouts and olives. Serve immediately.

Per serving: calories: 155, protein: 6 g, fat: 12 g, carbohydrate: 8 g, fiber: 3 g, sodium: 210 mg

This unlikely combination works! The avocado forms a creamy Alfredo-like sauce, and the chile and garlic add a kick.

pasta avocado

YIELD: 2 SERVINGS

2 zucchini, peeled

¾ **cup mashed avocados** (1½ avocados)

2 teaspoons minced jalapeño chile, or dash cayenne

½ teaspoon crushed garlic

¼ teaspoon salt

1 diced Roma tomato, for garnish

2 wedges lime, for garnish

EQUIPMENT

peeler

vegetable spiral slicer

medium bowl

fork

measuring cups

cutting board

chef's knife, 8-inch

measuring spoons

garlic press

rubber spatula

tongs

Cut the zucchini into thin noodles using a vegetable spiral slicer. Alternatively, use a vegetable peeler to create long ribbons, or "fettuccine," by drawing the peeler down all sides of the zucchini until you reach the core. Put the avocados, chile, garlic, and salt in a medium bowl and stir to combine. Add the zucchini noodles and toss. Serve immediately, garnished with the tomato and lime wedges.

Per serving: calories: 256, protein: 5 g, fat: 20 g, carbohydrate: 8 g, fiber: 11 g, sodium: 300 mg

This is a great on-the-go lunch that you can eat with your hands.

stuffed bell pepper

YIELD: 1 SERVING

½ **red bell pepper, seeded** (or ¼ red bell pepper, if large)

⅓ **cup Not Tuna Pâté** (page 71)**, Sunflower Seed–Herb Pâté** (page 73)**, or Guacamole** (page 67)

½ **teaspoon minced fresh parsley, for garnish**

EQUIPMENT

cutting board

chef's knife, 8-inch

paring knife

measuring cups

measuring spoons

spoon

Trim the white membranes from the pepper using a paring knife. Fill the pepper with the pâté. Garnish with the parsley. Serve immediately.

STUFFED TOMATO: Replace the bell pepper half with a whole tomato. To prepare the tomato for stuffing, cut out the section around the stem with a paring knife and remove. Insert a small measuring spoon into the hole and scoop out the seeds and membranes. Stuff with the pâté. Garnish with the parsley.

Per serving: calories: 181, protein: 6 g, fat: 15 g, carbohydrate: 8 g, fiber: 4 g, sodium: 231 mg

VEGETABLE SIDE DISHES

To make raw vegetables—such as beets, broccoli, cabbage, carrots, cauliflower, collard greens, and kale—more palatable, marinate them in a dressing of lemon juice, extra-virgin olive oil, and salt. This breaks down the fibers, just as cooking does, but without the loss of nutrients and flavors. When you marinate kale or collard greens, work the dressing into them with your hands. Also, the finer that you slice, shred, or chop the vegetables, the more readily they can be penetrated and softened by the marinade.

A nice accompaniment to California Rolls (page 134) or Not Tuna Rolls (page 134).

cucumbers with fresh mint

YIELD: 1 SERVING

1 cup peeled, seeded, and diced cucumber

¼ cup peeled and shredded carrot (optional)

1 tablespoon minced fresh mint

1 teaspoon freshly squeezed lemon juice

½ teaspoon extra-virgin olive oil

¼ teaspoon crushed garlic

⅛ teaspoon salt

Dash ground cumin

Dash ground pepper

Put all the ingredients in a medium bowl and toss to combine. Let sit for 5 to 10 minutes before serving to allow the flavors to meld. Stored in a sealed container in the refrigerator, Cucumbers with Fresh Mint will keep for 3 days.

EQUIPMENT

cutting board

peeler

spoon

chef's knife, 8-inch

measuring cups

grater, or food processor fitted with a shredding disk

measuring spoons

citrus juicer or reamer

garlic press

medium bowl

rubber spatula

Per serving: calories: 66, protein: 2 g, fat: 3 g, carbohydrate: 10 g, fiber: 2 g, sodium: 283 mg

This dish complements Zucchini Hummus (page 70) and Tabouli (page 152).

carrots with moroccan spices

SEE PHOTO BETWEEN PAGES 152 AND 153.

YIELD: 2 SERVINGS

2 carrots, peeled and thinly sliced

2 tablespoons chopped fresh parsley

2 tablespoons freshly squeezed orange juice

1½ teaspoons freshly squeezed lemon juice

1 teaspoon extra-virgin olive oil

⅛ teaspoon salt

Dash cayenne

Dash ground cinnamon

Dash ground cumin

Dash ground pepper

EQUIPMENT

cutting board

peeler

chef's knife, 8-inch

mandoline (optional, for slicing carrots)

measuring spoons

citrus juicer or reamer

medium bowl

saucepan (optional)

Put all the ingredients in a medium bowl. Toss with your hands until well combined, working the dressing into the carrots. Stored in a sealed container in the refrigerator, Carrots with Moroccan Spices will keep for 3 days.

WARMING OPTION: Put in a small saucepan over low heat and warm gently for 2 to 3 minutes. Do not overheat.

Per serving: calories: 58, protein: 1 g, fat: 2 g, carbohydrate: 7 g, fiber: 2 g, sodium: 191 mg

Please diners of all ages with this simple, refreshing salad. The savory lemon dressing balances the sweet carrots perfectly.

carrots with parsley and walnuts

YIELD: 1 SERVING

1 cup peeled and shredded carrots

2 tablespoons chopped fresh parsley

2 tablespoons chopped walnuts, unsoaked

2 teaspoons freshly squeezed lemon juice

1 teaspoon extra-virgin olive oil

⅛ teaspoon salt

Dash ground pepper (optional)

EQUIPMENT

cutting board

peeler

grater, or a food processor fitted
    with a shredding disk

measuring cups

chef's knife, 8-inch

measuring spoons

citrus juicer or reamer

medium bowl

rubber spatula

Put all the ingredients in a medium bowl and toss to combine. Stored in a sealed container in the refrigerator, Carrots with Parsley and Walnuts will keep for 3 days.

CARROTS WITH GOLDEN RAISINS AND FRESH MINT: Omit the parsley and walnuts. Add 2 tablespoons of golden raisins, soaked in water for 10 minutes (to plump and soften) and drained, and 2 tablespoons of chopped fresh mint.

Per serving: calories: 174, protein: 3 g, fat: 13 g, carbohydrate: 11 g, fiber: 4 g, sodium: 320 mg

This sweet-and-sour slaw is a delightful change from typical mayonnaise-laden versions.

coleslaw

YIELD: 1 SERVING

1½ cups thinly sliced green or red cabbage or a combination

⅛ teaspoon salt

¼ cup peeled and shredded carrot

6 thin slices red onion (optional)

2 teaspoons cider vinegar or freshly squeezed lemon juice

1 teaspoon agave nectar or maple syrup

1 teaspoon extra-virgin olive oil

¼ teaspoon celery seeds (optional)

Dash ground pepper

EQUIPMENT

cutting board

chef's knife, 8-inch

mandoline (optional, for thinly slicing cabbage and onion)

measuring cups

measuring spoons

medium bowl

peeler

grater, or food processor fitted with a shredding disk

rubber spatula

Put the cabbage and salt in a medium bowl. Massage the cabbage for about 1 minute with your hands to soften it. Add the carrot, optional onion, vinegar, agave nectar, oil, celery seeds, and pepper and toss until well combined. Stored in a sealed container in the refrigerator, Coleslaw will keep for 3 days.

Per serving: calories: 100, protein: 2 g, fat: 5 g, carbohydrate: 11 g, fiber: 4 g, sodium: 311 mg

This authentic Costa Rican dish tastes delicious with Guacamole (page 67) and Papaya-Lime Soup (page 88).

latin american cabbage

SEE PHOTO BETWEEN PAGES 152 AND 153.   **YIELD: 1 SERVING**

1½ cups thinly sliced green cabbage

⅛ teaspoon salt

½ tomato, seeded and diced

¼ cucumber, peeled, seeded, and thinly sliced

½ stalk celery, diced

¼ red bell pepper, diced

2 tablespoons minced fresh cilantro

1 tablespoon freshly squeezed lime juice

2 teaspoons minced onion

1 teaspoon extra-virgin olive oil

EQUIPMENT

cutting board

chef's knife, 8-inch

mandoline (optional, for thinly slicing cabbage)

measuring cups

measuring spoons

medium bowl

serrated knife, 5-inch

peeler

spoon

citrus juicer or reamer

tongs

Put the cabbage and salt in a medium bowl. Massage the cabbage for about 1 minute with your hands to soften it. Add the tomato, cucumber, celery, bell pepper, cilantro, lime juice, onion, and oil and toss until well combined. Stored in a sealed container in the refrigerator, Latin American Cabbage will keep for 2 days.

Per serving: calories: 105, protein: 3 g, fat: 5 g, carbohydrate: 11 g, fiber: 5 g, sodium: 320 mg

When kale is cut into thin strips and marinated in a dressing, it becomes soft and juicy.

mediterranean kale

SEE PHOTO BETWEEN PAGES 152 AND 153.   YIELD: 1 SERVING

4 leaves kale, stemmed

1½ teaspoons freshly squeezed lemon juice

1 teaspoon extra-virgin olive oil

⅛ teaspoon salt

¼ red bell pepper, diced

1 tablespoon pine nuts or chopped cashews

1 tablespoon sliced black olives

Dash ground pepper (optional)

EQUIPMENT

cutting board

chef's knife, 8-inch

medium bowl

citrus juicer or reamer

measuring spoons

serrated knife, 5-inch

tongs

saucepan (optional)

Stack two of the kale leaves with the stem end facing you. Fold in half lengthwise and roll tightly like a cigar. Slice crosswise into thin strips. Repeat with the remaining 2 leaves. Chop the kale strips a few times, so they aren't too long, and put them in a medium bowl. Add the lemon juice, oil, and salt. Toss well with your hands, working the dressing into the greens. Add the bell pepper, pine nuts, and olives and toss gently. Season with ground pepper if desired. Stored in a sealed container in the refrigerator, Mediterranean Kale will keep for 3 days. Bring to room temperature before serving.

WARMING OPTION: Put in a small saucepan over low heat and warm gently for 2 to 3 minutes. Do not overheat.

MEDITERRANEAN KALE WITH PINE NUTS AND DRIED FRUIT: Omit the bell pepper and olives. Add 1 tablespoon of golden raisins or dried cranberries.

MEDITERRANEAN PARSLEY: Replace the kale with 1 cup of minced fresh parsley. You do not need to work the dressing into the parsley with your hands; just toss everything together with a rubber spatula.

Per serving: calories: 180, protein: 5 g, fat: 13 g, carbohydrate: 11 g, fiber: 3 g, sodium: 385 mg

The sweet, creamy sauce makes this slaw luscious enough for dessert.

dilly slaw

YIELD: 1 SERVING

2 cups thinly sliced green
   cabbage

¼ cup Sweet Tahini Mayonnaise
(page 67)

1 tablespoon minced
   fresh dill

EQUIPMENT

cutting board

chef's knife, 8-inch

mandoline (optional, for
   thinly slicing cabbage)

measuring cups

measuring spoons

medium bowl

Put all the ingredients in a medium bowl. Massage for about 1 minute with your hands to soften the cabbage. Stored in a sealed container in the refrigerator, Dilly Slaw will keep for 24 hours.

Per serving: calories: 223, protein: 7 g, fat: 15 g, carbohydrate: 14 g, fiber: 7 g, sodium: 181 mg

Marinating broccoli and mushrooms makes them taste cooked—without the loss of nutrients.

marinated vegetables

YIELD: 1 SERVING

1 cup small broccoli florets

6 cremini mushrooms, quartered

½ cup peeled and thinly sliced
   carrot

1½ tablespoons Lemon-Herb
   Dressing (page 120)
   or Classic Vinaigrette
   (page 113)

EQUIPMENT

measuring cups

cutting board

chef's knife, 8-inch

peeler

measuring spoons

medium bowl

Put all the ingredients in a medium bowl. Toss well with your hands, working the dressing into the vegetables. Let marinate for 4 to 12 hours in the refrigerator before serving. Stored in a sealed container in the refrigerator, Marinated Vegetables will keep for 3 days. Bring to room temperature before serving.

Per serving: calories: 188, protein: 5 g, fat: 14 g, carbohydrate: 11 g, fiber: 2 g, sodium: 145 mg

Southern-style greens go raw. Massaging preserves their color and nutrition; garlic and cayenne keep their spicy kick.

southern greens

YIELD: 1 SERVING

4 leaves green or red curly kale or a
   combination, stemmed

2 leaves collard greens, stemmed

4 leaves basil, chopped

2 teaspoons freshly squeezed lemon juice

1 teaspoon extra-virgin olive oil

½ teaspoon crushed garlic

⅛ teaspoon salt

Dash cayenne

EQUIPMENT

cutting board

chef's knife, 8-inch

medium bowl

citrus juicer or reamer

measuring spoons

garlic press

saucepan (optional)

Chop the kale medium-fine and put in a medium bowl. To prepare the collard greens, stack the leaves with the stem end facing you. Fold in half lengthwise and roll tightly like a cigar. Slice crosswise into thin strips, then chop medium-fine and put in the bowl with the kale. Add the basil, lemon juice, oil, garlic, salt, and cayenne. Work the dressing into the greens with your hands. Stored in a sealed container in the refrigerator, Southern Greens will keep for 3 days. Bring to room temperature before serving.

WARMING OPTION: Put in a small saucepan over low heat and warm gently for 2 to 3 minutes. Do not overheat.

ASIAN GREENS: Replace the collard greens with 2 stalks of bok choy, thinly sliced crosswise. Omit the basil and salt and add ½ teaspoon of tamari and ¼ teaspoon of minced fresh ginger.

INDIAN GREENS: Replace the collard greens with 2 leaves of mustard greens, rolled and sliced as directed for the collard greens. Omit the basil and add a dash of ground cumin and a dash of curry powder.

Per serving: calories: 98, protein: 4 g, fat: 5 g, carbohydrate: 9 g, fiber: 3 g, sodium: 325 mg

My raw tabouli is lighter than the traditional bulgur wheat version of this fragrant Middle Eastern dish.

tabouli

YIELD: 1 SERVING

¾ cup minced fresh parsley, firmly packed

½ Roma tomato, seeded and diced

1 tablespoon minced fresh mint

1 tablespoon chopped green onion

1½ teaspoons freshly squeezed lemon juice

1 teaspoon extra-virgin olive oil

⅛ teaspoon salt

EQUIPMENT

cutting board

chef's knife, 8-inch

measuring cups

serrated knife, 5-inch

measuring spoons

citrus juicer or reamer

small bowl

rubber spatula

Put all the ingredients in a small bowl and toss to combine. Stored in a sealed container in the refrigerator, Tabouli will keep for 3 days.

Per serving: calories: 75, protein: 2 g, fat: 5 g, carbohydrate: 5 g, fiber: 3 g, sodium: 310 mg

Stuffed Mushroom, *page 138,* **with Sunflower Seed and Sun-Dried Tomato Pâté,** *page 73,* **Mediterranean Kale,** *page 149,* **and Carrots with Moroccan Spices,** *page 145*

Tropical Fruit Tart, *page 173*

This elegant preparation tastes like a cooked side dish you'd order at a fine Italian restaurant.

swiss chard with pine nuts and raisins

YIELD: 1 SERVING

4 leaves Swiss chard, stemmed

1½ teaspoons freshly squeezed lemon juice

1 teaspoon extra-virgin olive oil

⅛ teaspoon salt

1 tablespoon pine nuts or chopped cashews, unsoaked

1 tablespoon golden raisins, soaked in water for 10 minutes and drained

Dash ground pepper (optional)

EQUIPMENT

cutting board

chef's knife, 8-inch

citrus juicer or reamer

measuring spoons

medium bowl

small bowl

small colander or fine-mesh strainer

saucepan (optional)

Stack two of the Swiss chard leaves with the stem end facing you. Fold in half lengthwise and roll tightly like a cigar. Slice crosswise into thin strips. Repeat with the remaining 2 leaves. Chop the Swiss chard strips a few times, so they aren't too long, and put them in a medium bowl. Add the lemon juice, oil, and salt. Toss well with your hands, working the dressing into the greens. Add the pine nuts and raisins and toss gently. Season with ground pepper if desired. Stored in a sealed container in the refrigerator, Swiss Chard with Pine Nuts and Raisins will keep for 3 days. Bring to room temperature before serving.

WARMING OPTION: Put in a small saucepan over low heat and warm gently for 2 to 3 minutes. Do not overheat.

Per serving: calories: 150, protein: 3 g, fat: 11 g, carbohydrate: 11 g, fiber: 2 g, sodium: 394 mg

RAW ON THE GO

Traveling can challenge your healthful routine. In airports and on the road, nutritious food is often unavailable. And eating out three times a day usually means fewer fresh fruits and vegetables and more fatty foods, starches, and desserts than you eat at home. But it doesn't have to be this way. You *can* come back from a trip healthy and energized. It just takes a little planning. The following tips will help you feel your best while traveling, and after you return home.

The first challenge is the travel day itself, whether you go by plane, car, bus, or train. Eat a good breakfast before you leave. If time is tight, prepare a green juice (pages 23 and 24) or a green smoothie (pages 39 through 50) the night before. Take along a few snacks, such as fresh fruit, raw veggies, and nuts or trail mix (see page 61), to tide you over until the next meal. Better yet, pack a salad and some Not Tuna Pâté (page 71) or Walnut Pâté (page 72).

When eating out during your travels, don't leave the hotel starving—have some fruit or another snack beforehand. In restaurants, keep it raw by ordering one or more salads. At Italian and French restaurants, dress salads with extra-virgin olive oil plus a squeeze of fresh lemon. At Mexican restaurants, add salsa and guacamole to turn a salad into a meal. And at Japanese restaurants, order all-veggie sushi rolls; just ask the chef to omit the fish and rice. When eating cooked food, good choices are steamed vegetables (instead of pasta) with marinara sauce, beans or lentils, and vegetable soups. Most restaurants will be flexible and allow you to mix and match from their menus or make substitutions.

If you want to go a step further, prepare some of your meals in the comfort of your hotel room. That's the advantage of traveling raw—you don't need a stove. And packing your own equipment and ingredients is not difficult. The gear can all fit into a small checked bag. Here is a comprehensive list of what to take with you. See Glossary, page 199, for more information on particular ingredients and equipment.

Raw Travel Gear

bamboo sushi mat (optional)

bowl, lightweight and large (for both mixing and eating)

bowl, lightweight and small (for eating)

chopping mat, flexible

container for leftovers, plastic

dish cloth in a ziplock bag

dish soap, small bottle

dish towel

fork and spoon

garlic press (optional)

knife, small, with a sheath

Mason jars, 2 (one pint-sized, one quart-sized)

measuring cups and spoons (optional)

peeler

plate, lightweight

sponge in a ziplock bag

travel blender and extension cord (optional)

vegetable spiral slicer (optional)

water bottle

Raw Travel Shopping List

PANTRY ITEMS

almond butter (homemade, page 78, or store-bought)

almonds

cinnamon, ground (optional)

dulse leaves or flakes (optional)

extra-virgin olive oil, small bottle (optional)

flaxseeds, ground

green powder (optional)

Ground Seed Mix (page 57; optional)

hempseeds (optional)

medjool dates

miso (optional)

nori (optional)

protein powder, raw vegan (optional)

salt

spirulina or chlorella (optional)

stevia, liquid (optional)

tea bags, herbal (optional)

trail mix (see page 61)

Fresh Produce

Buy the fresh ingredients on this list at your destination. When booking your hotel room, request one that has a small refrigerator.

apples

avocados

baby spinach

bananas

blueberries (fresh or frozen, if you have access to a freezer)

carrots

cucumbers

garlic (optional)

guacamole (homemade, page 67, or store-bought; optional)

lemons

mesclun

oranges

red bell peppers

romaine hearts

salsa (homemade, page 76, or store-bought; optional)

tomatoes

Raw Travel Menus

Here are some ideas for putting it all together.

Breakfast

Start the day with water, then have some more with spirulina or chlorella, shaken up in a pint-sized Mason jar. For the simplest breakfast, enjoy some fresh fruit. Or, use a travel blender to make Apple-Banana Green Smoothie (page 39) or Blueberry Green Smoothie (page 41), using spinach or green powder as the green. Add a tablespoon of ground flaxseeds or Ground Seed Mix (page 57) and a tablespoon of raw vegan protein powder to the smoothie if you like. For a cereal breakfast, have Multiseed Porridge (page 54) with Hemp Milk (page 57), which you can prepare in a travel blender. If you prefer a savory breakfast, an avocado is tasty and satisfying. Simply cut it in half, remove the pit, sprinkle the flesh with salt, and eat with a spoon.

Lunch

Prepare Garden Salad (page 94), including lettuce, spinach, tomato, cucumber, carrot, and avocado. Add some dulse flakes if you like. Dress with freshly squeezed lemon juice, extra-virgin olive oil, garlic, and salt. If you have a sweet tooth after your salad, enjoy a banana or some dates.

As an alternative to salad, make a wrap by filling romaine lettuce leaves with sliced avocado, tomato, and cucumber, or with guacamole and salsa. For a sweet wrap, spread the lettuce leaves with almond butter and banana slices.

Snacks

For quick satisfaction, have a piece of fresh fruit, some almonds and dates, or trail mix. For a veggie-based snack, make Crudités (page 91), using carrots, cucumber, and red bell pepper. Serve plain or with almond butter, guacamole, or salsa.

Dinner

Often you'll want to eat dinner out when traveling, but to dine in, you can make a delicious raw meal. California Rolls (page 134) are easy to make with a bamboo sushi mat. Spread the nori with miso and fill the rolls with carrot, cucumber, red bell pepper, and avocado. If you own a vegetable spiral slicer, use it to make zucchini noodles. Or just use a vegetable peeler to create long ribbons, or "fettuccine," by drawing the peeler down all sides of the zucchini until you reach the core. For an Italian meal, serve the noodles with diced tomato, extra-virgin olive oil, garlic, and salt.

desserts

All kinds of classic desserts—cake, cookies, fruit crisps, pies, tarts, puddings, mousses, shakes, and ice creams—can be dairy- and gluten-free. Raw desserts use ingredients made from whole foods, such as nuts, dried fruits, and avocados, to replace unhealthful white flour, white sugar, dairy products, and heated fats. Try Chocolate Mousse (page 180) for an elegant finale to lunch or dinner, Almond Cookies (page 164) or Brownies (page 166) with Almond Milk (page 58) as an afternoon snack, or a slice of Tropical Fruit Pie or Tart (page 173) as a light meal itself. Most of the recipes in this section provide more than two servings, so they're perfect for sharing with friends. See my book *Raw for Dessert* for even more recipes.

CAKES, COOKIES, AND BARS

Raw cakes, cookies, and bars are made from nuts, dried fruits, and flavorings such as cocoa, carob, citrus zest, and extracts. For the best texture, use unsoaked nuts and dried fruits. There's no need for cake pans or cookie sheets—these delicious no-bake desserts require only a food processor. To make a larger cake or batch of cookies, just double or triple the recipe.

This rich, fudgy cake couldn't be easier, yet it's elegant enough for any party.

walnut-raisin cake

YIELD: ONE 5-INCH CAKE, 6 SERVINGS

1 cup walnuts, unsoaked

1 cup raisins, unsoaked

¼ cup **Lemon Glaze or Orange Glaze** (page 184)

½ cup **fresh raspberries**

EQUIPMENT

measuring cups

food processor

rubber spatula

serving plate

Put the walnuts and raisins in a food processor fitted with the S blade and process until the mixture sticks together. Transfer to a serving plate and form into a cake, 5 inches in diameter. Frost the top and sides with the glaze. Refrigerate for at least 1 hour. Decorate the cake and plate with fresh raspberries before serving. Covered with plastic wrap, Walnut-Raisin Cake will keep for 5 days in the refrigerator or 2 weeks in the freezer. Serve chilled or at room temperature.

Per serving: calories: 218, protein: 4 g, fat: 11 g, carbohydrate: 28 g, fiber: 4 g, sodium: 4 mg

This scrumptious "coffee cake" has a crumble topping and a drizzle of white icing.

apple crumb cake

YIELD: ONE 5-INCH CAKE, 6 SERVINGS

¾ cup dried apples, firmly packed, unsoaked

3 pitted medjool dates, unsoaked

1 apple, peeled and shredded

⅛ teaspoon ground cinnamon

1 cup **Crumble Topping** (page 168)

2 tablespoons **Vanilla Crème Sauce** (page 185)

EQUIPMENT

measuring cups

cutting board

peeler

chef's knife, 8-inch

grater, or food processor fitted with a
    shredding disk

measuring spoons

food processor

rubber spatula

serving plate

Put the dried apples in a food processor fitted with the S blade and process until ground. Add the dates and process until finely chopped. Add the shredded apple and cinnamon and process until well combined, stopping occasionally to scrape down the work bowl with a rubber spatula.

Put ½ cup of the topping on a serving plate and shape it into a 5-inch circle. Put the apple mixture on top and form it into a cake, following the edges of the topping. Put the remaining topping over and around the sides of the cake. Refrigerate for at least 1 hour. Drizzle with the sauce before serving. Covered with plastic wrap and stored in the refrigerator, Apple Crumb Cake will keep for 3 days. Bring to room temperature before serving.

Per serving: calories: 275, protein: 4 g, fat: 19 g, carbohydrate: 24 g, fiber: 5 g, sodium: 59 mg

This Spanish confection is traditionally served in thin wedges with fruit for a snack or dessert.

spanish fig cake

YIELD: ONE 5-INCH CAKE, 6 SERVINGS

¾ **cup dried black Mission or calimyrna figs, unsoaked**

½ **cup almonds, unsoaked**

¼ **cup walnuts, unsoaked**

½ **cup fresh berries** (blueberries, blackberries, raspberries or a combination; optional)

EQUIPMENT

cutting board

paring knife

measuring cups

food processor

rubber spatula

serving plate

Trim the stems off the figs with a paring knife. Put the almonds and walnuts in a food processor fitted with the S blade and process until coarsely chopped. Add the figs and process until the mixture sticks together. Transfer to a serving plate and form into a cake, 5 inches in diameter. Decorate the cake and plate with fresh berries before serving if desired. Covered with plastic wrap, Spanish Fig Cake will keep for 3 days in the refrigerator or 2 weeks in the freezer. Bring to room temperature before serving.

SPANISH DATE CAKE: Replace the figs with pitted medjool dates, unsoaked.

Per serving: calories: 158, protein: 4 g, fat: 9 g, carbohydrate: 17 g, fiber: 4 g, sodium: 3 mg

This decadent dessert will delight chocolate lovers.

flourless chocolate cake

SEE PHOTO FACING PAGE 185.

YIELD: ONE 5-INCH CAKE, 6 SERVINGS

1½ cups walnuts or pecans, unsoaked

Dash salt

8 pitted medjool dates, unsoaked

⅓ cup unsweetened cocoa or carob powder

½ teaspoon vanilla extract

2 teaspoons water

½ cup fresh raspberries, for garnish

EQUIPMENT

measuring cups

food processor

measuring spoons

rubber spatula

serving plate

Put the walnuts and salt in a food processor fitted with the S blade and process until finely ground. Add the dates, cocoa powder, and vanilla extract and process until the mixture begins to stick together. Add the water and process briefly. Transfer to a serving plate and form into a cake, 5 inches in diameter. Decorate the cake and plate with fresh raspberries before serving if desired. Covered with plastic wrap, Flourless Chocolate Cake will keep for 3 days in the refrigerator or 2 weeks in the freezer. Bring to room temperature before serving.

BLACK FOREST CAKE: Top the cake with ¾ cup of pitted fresh or thawed and drained frozen cherries. Drizzle with 2 tablespoons of Vanilla Crème Sauce (page 185).

CHOCOLATE LAYER CAKE WITH RASPBERRY FILLING AND CHOCOLATE BUTTERCREAM FROSTING: Double the recipe to make two 5-inch cakes. Frost the top of one cake with ¼ cup of Raspberry Sauce (page 186). Put the other cake on top and frost the top and sides with ½ cup of Chocolate Buttercream Frosting (page 180). Refrigerate for at least 1 hour before serving. Yield: 6 to 8 servings.

FLOURLESS CHOCOLATE CAKE WITH RASPBERRY SAUCE: Serve each slice of cake with 2 tablespoons of Raspberry Sauce (page 186).

Per serving: calories: 207, protein: 5 g, fat: 17 g, carbohydrate: 12 g, fiber: 4 g, sodium: 2 mg

My raw "peanut butter" cookies use almond or cashew butter.

not peanut butter cookies

YIELD: 8 COOKIES, 4 SERVINGS

½ **cup raw almond or cashew butter** (preferably homemade, page 78)

¼ **cup maple syrup or agave nectar**

½ **teaspoon vanilla extract**

Dash salt

½ **cup Almond Flour** (page 165)

EQUIPMENT

measuring cups

measuring spoons

food processor

rubber spatula

small bowl

Put the almond butter, maple syrup, vanilla extract, and salt in a food processor fitted with the S blade and process until smooth. Transfer to a small bowl and put in the freezer for 30 minutes.

Scoop about 1 tablespoon of the almond butter mixture into your hand and squeeze until it sticks together. Roll into a 1-inch ball and flatten slightly to make a cookie. Repeat until you have used up all the almond butter mixture. Roll each cookie in the almond flour. Put in the freezer for at least 2 hours before serving. Stored in a sealed container in the freezer, Not Peanut Butter Cookies will keep for 1 month.

Per serving: calories: 232, protein: 7 g, fat: 16 g, carbohydrate: 20 g, fiber: 4 g, sodium: 24 mg

Watch out! This mixture tastes so good, you'll find yourself eating it straight out of the bowl.

almond cookies

SEE PHOTO FACING PAGE 184.   YIELD: 12 COOKIES, 4 SERVINGS

½ cup almonds, unsoaked

¼ cup walnuts or pecans, unsoaked

Dash salt

⅓ cup pitted medjool dates, unsoaked

¼ teaspoon almond extract

¼ cup raisins or dried cherries, unsoaked (optional)

¼ cup Almond Flour (page 165)

EQUIPMENT

measuring cups

food processor

measuring spoons

small bowl

rubber spatula

serving plate

Put the almonds, walnuts, and salt in a food processor fitted with the S blade and process until coarsely chopped. Add the dates and almond extract and process until the mixture begins to stick together. Don't overprocess; you should still see chunks of almonds and walnuts. Add the raisins if desired and pulse briefly, just to mix. Transfer to a small bowl.

Scoop about 1 tablespoon of the almond mixture into your hand and squeeze firmly until it sticks together. Roll into a 1-inch ball and flatten slightly to make a cookie. Repeat until you have used up all the almond mixture. Roll each cookie in the almond flour and put on a plate. Refrigerate for at least 1 hour before serving. Stored in a sealed container, Almond Cookies will keep for 1 month in the refrigerator or 3 months in the freezer.

CHOCOLATE CHIP COOKIES: Replace the raisins with chocolate or carob chips and add 1 teaspoon of orange zest if desired.

LEMON COOKIES: Replace the almond extract with lemon extract and add 1 teaspoon of lemon zest.

SCHOOLBOY COOKIES: Omit the raisins and press a small square of dark chocolate onto the top of each cookie.

Per serving: calories: 137, protein: 5 g, fat: 12 g, carbohydrate: 5 g, fiber: 3 g, sodium: 22 mg

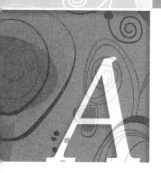

Ground almonds can be used to replace flour in raw cakes, cookies, and pie crusts.

almond flour

YIELD: 1¼ CUPS

1 cup almonds, unsoaked

EQUIPMENT
measuring cups
food processor
rubber spatula

Put the almonds in a food processor fitted with the S blade and process until finely ground. Stored in a sealed container, Almond Flour will keep for 1 month in the refrigerator or 3 months in the freezer.

Per ¼ cup: calories: 164, protein: 6 g, fat: 15 g, carbohydrate: 6 g, fiber: 3 g, sodium: 0 mg

This easy recipe tastes remarkably like conventional chocolate chip cookie dough. Eat it by the spoonful or the handful, as your yearning dictates.

chocolate chip cookie dough

YIELD: 2 CUPS, 8 SERVINGS

1½ cups cashews, unsoaked
⅛ teaspoon salt
¾ cup pitted medjool dates, unsoaked
½ cup chocolate chips

EQUIPMENT
measuring cups
measuring spoons
food processor
small bowl

Put the cashews and salt in a food processor fitted with the S blade and process until coarsely ground. Add the dates and process until the mixture begins to stick together. Add the chocolate chips and pulse briefly, just to mix. Transfer to a small bowl to serve. Stored in a sealed container, Chocolate Chip Cookie Dough will keep for 1 month in the refrigerator or 3 months in the freezer.

Per serving: calories: 258, protein: 6 g, fat: 16 g, carbohydrate: 25 g, fiber: 2 g, sodium: 39 mg

Delicious, moist, and ready in just five minutes.

brownies

YIELD: 8 BROWNIES, 8 SERVINGS

1½ cups walnuts or pecans, unsoaked

Dash salt

8 pitted medjool dates, unsoaked

⅓ cup unsweetened cocoa or carob powder

½ teaspoon vanilla or cherry extract (optional)

2 teaspoons water

¼ cup chopped dried cherries (optional)

EQUIPMENT

measuring cups

cutting board

chef's knife, 8-inch

measuring spoons

food processor

rubber spatula

small bowl

6-inch square glass container (such as a container used for leftovers)

Chop ¼ cup of the walnuts and set aside. Put the remaining 1¼ cups of walnuts and the salt in a food processor fitted with the S blade and process until finely ground. Add the dates and process until the mixture sticks together. Add the cocoa powder and optional vanilla extract and process until evenly distributed. Add the water and process briefly. Transfer to a small bowl. Add the reserved chopped walnuts and optional dried cherries and mix well using your hands. Pack the mixture firmly into a 6-inch square glass container. Stored in a sealed container, Brownies will keep for 1 week in the refrigerator or 1 month in the freezer.

CHOCOLATE CHIP BROWNIES: Replace the dried cherries with chocolate chips.

Per serving: calories: 154, protein: 4 g, fat: 13 g, carbohydrate: 9 g, fiber: 3 g, sodium: 1 mg

CRISPS, PIES, AND TARTS

Raw pie and tart crusts are made from nuts, coconut, and salt, which provide a buttery taste, plus dates, which bind the crust ingredients together. Crisps are made with Crumble Topping (page 168), a sweet mixture of ground nuts, dates, raisins, and spices. Fruit fillings for these desserts use fresh and dried fruits; creamy fillings feature avocados (once you add flavorings, such as agave nectar, cocoa, or lime juice, no one will suspect that avocados provide the smooth texture). To make a tart instead of a pie, use a tart pan with a removable bottom. After filling the crust, push up on the bottom to release the tart from the pan.

Raw pie and tart dough is not rolled out; it is shaped with your hands. To form the crust, simply scoop the crumbly dough into the pan. Use a light circular motion with your palm and fingers to distribute the crumbs uniformly along the bottom and up the sides of the pan. There should be a three-quarter-inch lip of crumbs along the sides. After the crumbs are evenly distributed, press the crust down on the bottom of the pan using your fingers and palm. Be sure to press especially firmly where the bottom of the pan joins the sides. Then press the crust against the pan's sides, shaping it so that its edges are flush with the rim.

The recipes in this section provide standard-sized crisps, pies, and tarts that serve eight, but you can make individual crisps and tarts as well. Just divide any crust and filling recipes in half and use ramekins or small bowls for individual crisps or five-inch tart pans for miniature tarts. You can freeze any leftover crust for future use and eat extra fruit fillings for breakfasts and snacks.

167

This topping tastes freshly baked! Use it on crisps, as a crust for Apple Crumb Cake (page 160), or eat it straight.

crumble topping

YIELD: 2 CUPS, 12 SERVINGS

2 cups walnuts or pecans, unsoaked

½ cup unsweetened shredded dried coconut

¼ teaspoon ground cinnamon

¼ teaspoon ground nutmeg

¼ teaspoon salt

8 pitted medjool dates, unsoaked

½ cup raisins, unsoaked

¼ cup whole cane sugar, coconut sugar, or maple sugar (optional, for a sweeter topping)

EQUIPMENT

measuring cups

measuring spoons

food processor

rubber spatula

Put the walnuts, coconut, cinnamon, nutmeg, and salt in a food processor fitted with the S blade and process until coarsely ground. Add the dates and raisins and process until the mixture breaks down into coarse crumbs and begins to stick together. Don't overprocess. Add the optional sugar and process briefly. Stored in a sealed container, Crumble Topping will keep for 1 month in the refrigerator or 3 months in the freezer.

Per serving (based on 8 servings): calories: 207, protein: 4 g, fat: 17 g, carbohydrate: 12 g, fiber: 3 g, sodium: 49 mg

With a honey-sweet flavor and a subtle seedy crunch, dried figs are a great alternative to dates in raw crusts. For fall, try this crust with Apple Pie (page 175).

fig crust

YIELD: 3 CUPS, FOR ONE 9-INCH PIE OR TART CRUST

1⅓ cups dried black Mission figs, unsoaked

2 cups pecans, unsoaked

EQUIPMENT

cutting board

paring knife

measuring cups

food processor

rubber spatula

Trim off the stems of the figs with a paring knife. Put the pecans in a food processor fitted with the S blade. Add the figs and process until the mixture sticks together. Stored in a sealed container, Fig Crust will keep for 2 weeks in the refrigerator or 1 month in the freezer.

Per serving (based on 8 servings): calories: 279, protein: 4 g, fat: 21 g, carbohydrate: 19 g, fiber: 6 g, sodium: 3 mg

This delicately flavored crust enhances any pie or tart filling.

almond crust

YIELD: 3 CUPS, FOR ONE 9-INCH PIE OR TART CRUST

2¼ cups Almond Flour (page 165)

¾ cup pitted medjool dates, unsoaked

¼ teaspoon salt

EQUIPMENT

measuring cups

measuring spoons

food processor

rubber spatula

Put all the ingredients in a food processor fitted with the S blade and process until the mixture breaks down into coarse crumbs and begins to stick together. Don't overprocess. Stored in a sealed container, Almond Crust will keep for 1 month in the refrigerator or 3 months in the freezer.

Per serving (based on 8 servings): calories: 232, protein: 7 g, fat: 16 g, carbohydrate: 18 g, fiber: 5 g, sodium: 67 mg

Walnuts add vitamin E and omega-3 fatty acids to a healthful diet. This recipe combines them with dried coconut for an elegant, buttery crust.

walnut crust

YIELD: 3 CUPS, FOR ONE 9-INCH PIE OR TART CRUST

2 cups walnuts or pecans, unsoaked

1 cup unsweetened shredded dried coconut

¼ teaspoon salt

½ cup pitted medjool dates, unsoaked

EQUIPMENT

measuring cups

measuring spoons

food processor

rubber spatula

Put the walnuts, coconut, and salt in a food processor fitted with the S blade and process until coarsely ground. Add the dates and process until the mixture breaks down into coarse crumbs and begins to stick together. Don't overprocess. Stored in a sealed container, Walnut Crust will keep for 1 month in the refrigerator or 3 months in the freezer.

Per serving (based on 8 servings): calories: 262, protein: 5 g, fat: 23 g, carbohydrate: 14 g, fiber: 4 g, sodium: 71 mg

Serve plain or with Vanilla Crème Sauce (page 185) or Vanilla Ice Cream (page 191).

apple crisp

YIELD: ONE 8-INCH CRISP, 12 SERVINGS

4 apples, peeled

3 tablespoons freshly squeezed lemon juice

½ cup pitted medjool dates, soaked in water for 10 minutes and drained

½ cup raisins, soaked in water for 10 minutes and drained

¼ teaspoon ground cinnamon

2 cups Crumble Topping (page 168)

EQUIPMENT

cutting board

peeler

chef's knife, 8-inch

paring knife

citrus juicer or reamer

measuring spoons

medium bowl

rubber spatula

measuring cups

small bowls, two

small colander or fine-mesh strainer

food processor

baking dish, glass, 8-inch square

Thinly slice 2 of the apples and chop the remaining 2 apples. Put the sliced apples and 2 tablespoons of the lemon juice in a medium bowl. Toss gently and set aside. Put the chopped apples, dates, raisins, cinnamon, and remaining tablespoon of lemon juice in a food processor fitted with the S blade and process until smooth. Add to the sliced apples, stirring until well combined.

To assemble the crisp, press ½ cup of the topping into an even layer in an 8-inch square glass baking dish. Spread the apple filling on top using a rubber spatula. With your hands, knead pieces of the remaining 1½ cups of topping until they stick together. Lay these pieces of topping on the filling to form a cobbled appearance, allowing some of the filling to peek through. Serve chilled, at room temperature, or warm (see warming option). Covered with plastic wrap and stored in the refrigerator, Apple Crisp will keep for 3 days.

WARMING OPTION: Preheat the oven to 200 degrees F. Turn off the oven, insert the crisp, and warm for 15 minutes. Alternatively, heat for 30 minutes in a food dehydrator set at 105 degrees F.

Per serving: calories: 200, protein: 3 g, fat: 11 g, carbohydrate: 23 g, fiber: 4 g, sodium: 34 mg

Tart, juicy blackberries are a delight under this sweet, crumbly topping. Try Blackberry Crisp warm, with a scoop of Vanilla Ice Cream (page 191).

blackberry crisp

SEE PHOTO FACING PAGE 184.

YIELD: ONE 8-INCH CRISP, 12 SERVINGS

4 cups fresh or thawed and drained frozen blackberries

¾ cup pitted medjool dates, soaked in water for 10 minutes and drained

1 tablespoon freshly squeezed lemon juice

2 cups Crumble Topping (page 168)

EQUIPMENT

measuring cups

small bowl

small colander or fine-mesh strainer

citrus juicer or reamer

measuring spoons

food processor

rubber spatula

medium bowl

square pan, glass, 8-inch

Put 1½ cups of the blackberries along with the dates and lemon juice in a food processor fitted with the S blade and process until smooth. Transfer to a medium bowl, add the remaining 2½ cups of blackberries, and stir gently until well combined.

To assemble the crisp, press ½ cup of the topping into an even layer in an 8-inch square glass baking dish. Spread the blackberry filling on top using a rubber spatula. With your hands, knead pieces of the remaining 1½ cups of the topping until they stick together. Lay these pieces of topping on the filling to form a cobbled appearance, allowing some of the filling to peek through. Refrigerate for at least 1 hour before serving. Serve chilled, at room temperature, or warm (see warming option). Covered with plastic wrap and stored in the refrigerator, Blackberry Crisp will keep for 3 days.

WARMING OPTION: Preheat the oven to 200 degrees F. Turn off the oven, insert the crisp, and warm for 15 minutes. Alternatively, heat for 30 minutes in a food dehydrator set at 105 degrees F.

BLUEBERRY OR CHERRY CRISP: Replace the blackberries with 4 cups of fresh or thawed and drained frozen blueberries or pitted cherries.

PEACH CRISP: Replace the blackberries with 4 cups of fresh or thawed frozen peach slices. Add ⅛ teaspoon of ground nutmeg to the filling if desired.

Per serving: calories: 191, protein: 3 g, fat: 12 g, carbohydrate: 17 g, fiber: 6 g, sodium: 34 mg

This light, fruity tart is the perfect ending to an Asian or Latin American meal.

tropical fruit pie or tart

SEE PHOTO FACING PAGE 153.

YIELD: ONE 9-INCH PIE OR TART, 8 SERVINGS

3 cups **Walnut Crust** (page 170)

2 cups **Mango Pudding or Pineapple Pudding** (page 183)

2 cups fresh raspberries

1 cup fresh blackberries

1 cup fresh blueberries

EQUIPMENT

measuring cups

pie plate, or tart pan with removable bottom, 9-inch

rubber spatula

medium bowl

Scoop the crust into a pie or tart pan. Use a light circular motion with your palm and fingers to distribute the crumbs uniformly along the bottom and up the sides of the pan. There should be a ¾-inch lip of crumbs along the sides. After the crumbs are evenly distributed, press the crust down on the bottom of the pan using your fingers and palm. Be sure to press especially firmly where the bottom of the pan joins the sides. Then press the crust against the pan's sides, shaping it so that the edges are flush with the rim. Put the crust in the freezer for 15 minutes.

Remove the crust from the freezer and spread the pudding over the bottom. Put the raspberries, blackberries, and blueberries in a medium bowl and toss gently. Arrange the berries over the top of the tart so that the entire tart is covered. Refrigerate for at least 1 hour before serving. Serve chilled or at room temperature. Covered with plastic wrap and stored in the refrigerator, Tropical Fruit Pie or Tart will keep for 3 days.

Per serving: calories: 461, protein: 8 g, fat: 24 g, carbohydrate: 59 g, fiber: 11 g, sodium: 73 mg

This tart has a bright green filling and is topped with rainbow-colored rings of fruit, making it as stunning as it is delicious.

key lime pie or tart

YIELD: ONE 9-INCH PIE OR TART, 8 SERVINGS

3 cups Walnut Crust (page 170)

2 cups Key Lime Mousse (page 179)

3 kiwifruit, peeled

2 cups fresh raspberries

1 cup fresh blueberries

EQUIPMENT

measuring cups

pie plate, or tart pan with removable bottom, 9-inch

rubber spatula

cutting board

paring knife

KEY LIME SHERBET TART: After spreading the mousse over the crust, put the tart in the freezer for at least 2 hours. Thaw for 10 minutes before serving. To serve the entire tart, top with the fresh fruit and serve immediately. To serve a portion of the tart, cut individual slices and top each with fresh fruit before serving. Refreeze the rest of the tart; covered with plastic wrap, it will keep for 2 weeks.

Scoop the crust into a pie or tart pan. Use a light circular motion with your palm and fingers to distribute the crumbs uniformly along the bottom and up the sides of the pan. There should be a ¾-inch lip of crumbs along the sides. After the crumbs are evenly distributed, press the crust down on the bottom of the pan using your fingers and palm. Be sure to press especially firmly where the bottom of the pan joins the sides. Then press the crust against the pan's sides, shaping it so that the edges are flush with the rim. Put the crust in the freezer for 15 minutes.

Remove the crust from the freezer and spread the mousse over the bottom. Cut the kiwifruit in half lengthwise, then slice the halves into half-moons. Arrange the slices around the outer edge of the tart, propping them at an angle against the crust. Arrange the raspberries in two more rings inside the ring of kiwifruit slices. Mound the blueberries in the center of the tart. Refrigerate for at least 1 hour before serving. Serve chilled or at room temperature. Covered with plastic wrap and stored in the refrigerator, Key Lime Pie or Tart will keep for 3 days.

Per serving: calories: 475, protein: 7 g, fat: 33 g, carbohydrate: 39 g, fiber: 13 g, sodium: 77 mg

Dates, raisins, and cinnamon give this pie sweetness and depth. Serve plain or with Vanilla Crème Sauce (page 185).

apple pie or tart

3 cups **Almond Crust** (page 169), **Fig Crust** (page 169), or **Walnut Crust** (page 170)

4 apples, peeled

3 tablespoons freshly squeezed lemon juice

½ cup pitted medjool dates, soaked in water for 10 minutes and drained

½ cup raisins, soaked in water for 10 minutes and drained

¼ teaspoon ground cinnamon

EQUIPMENT

measuring cups

pie plate, or tart pan with removable bottom, 9-inch

cutting board

peeler

paring knife

citrus juicer or reamer

measuring spoons

medium bowl

small bowls, two

small colander or fine-mesh strainer

food processor

rubber spatula

Per serving: calories: 327, protein: 8 g, fat: 17 g, carbohydrate: 41 g, fiber: 7 g, sodium: 69 mg

Scoop the crust into a pie plate or tart pan. Use a light circular motion with your palm and fingers to distribute the crumbs uniformly along the bottom and up the sides of the pan. There should be a ¾-inch lip of crumbs along the sides. After the crumbs are evenly distributed, press the crust down on the bottom of the pan using your fingers and palm. Be sure to press especially firmly where the bottom of the pan joins the sides. Then press the crust against the pan's sides, shaping it so that its edges are flush with the rim. Put the crust in the freezer for 15 minutes.

Thinly slice 2 of the apples and chop the remaining 2 apples. Put the sliced apples and 2 tablespoons of the lemon juice in a medium bowl. Toss gently and set aside. Put the chopped apples, dates, raisins, cinnamon, and remaining tablespoon of lemon juice in a food processor fitted with the S blade and process until smooth. Add to the sliced apples, stirring until well combined.

Remove the crust from the freezer. Add the apple filling and press down with a rubber spatula. Serve chilled, at room temperature, or warm (see warming option). Covered with plastic wrap and stored in the refrigerator, Apple Pie or Tart will keep for 3 days.

WARMING OPTION: Preheat the oven to 200 degrees F. Turn off the oven, insert the pie, and warm for 15 minutes. Alternatively, heat for 30 minutes in a food dehydrator set at 105 degrees F.

Forget cornstarch and sugar—dates thicken and sweeten the blueberry filling in this pie.

blueberry pie or tart

YIELD: ONE 9-INCH PIE OR TART, 8 SERVINGS

3 cups Almond Crust (page 169) **or Walnut Crust** (page 170)

4 cups fresh or thawed and drained frozen blueberries

¾ cup pitted medjool dates, soaked in water for 10 minutes and drained

1 tablespoon freshly squeezed lemon juice

EQUIPMENT

measuring cups

pie plate, or tart pan with removable bottom, 9-inch

small colander or fine-mesh strainer

small bowl

citrus juicer or reamer

measuring spoons

blender

rubber spatula

medium bowl

Per serving: calories: 321, protein: 8 g, fat: 17 g, carbohydrate: 38 g, fiber: 8 g, sodium: 68 mg

Scoop the crust into a pie plate or tart pan. Use a light circular motion with your palm and fingers to distribute the crumbs uniformly along the bottom and up the sides of the pan. There should be a ¾-inch lip of crumbs along the sides. After the crumbs are evenly distributed, press the crust down on the bottom of the pan using your fingers and palm. Be sure to press especially firmly where the bottom of the pan joins the sides. Then press the crust against the pan's sides, shaping it so that its edges are flush with the rim. Put the crust in the freezer for 15 minutes.

Put 1½ cups of the blueberries along with the dates and lemon juice in a blender and process until smooth. Transfer to a medium bowl, add the remaining blueberries, and stir gently until well combined.

Remove the crust from the freezer. Add the blueberry filling and press down with a rubber spatula. Refrigerate for at least 1 hour before serving. Serve chilled, at room temperature, or warm (see page 8). Covered with plastic wrap and stored in the refrigerator, Blueberry Pie or Tart will keep for 3 days.

BLACKBERRY OR CHERRY PIE OR TART: Replace the blueberries with 4 cups of fresh or thawed and drained frozen blackberries or pitted cherries.

PEACH PIE OR TART: Replace the blueberries with 4 cups of fresh or thawed frozen peach slices. Add ⅛ teaspoon of ground nutmeg to the filling if desired.

This beautiful and luscious tart pairs fluffy chocolate filling with sweet juicy berries.

chocolate pie or tart with strawberries

YIELD: ONE 9-INCH PIE OR TART, 8 SERVINGS

3 cups Almond Crust (page 169) **or Walnut Crust** (page 170)

2 cups Chocolate Mousse (page 180)

1 pound fresh strawberries, hulled and thinly sliced

EQUIPMENT

measuring cups

pie plate, or tart pan with removable bottom, 9-inch

rubber spatula

cutting board

paring knife

Scoop the crust into a pie plate or tart pan. Use a light circular motion with your palm and fingers to distribute the crumbs uniformly along the bottom and up the sides of the pan. There should be a ¾-inch lip of crumbs along the sides. After the crumbs are evenly distributed, press the crust down on the bottom of the pan using your fingers and palm. Be sure to press especially firmly where the bottom of the pan joins the sides. Then press the crust against the pan's sides, shaping it so that the edges are flush with the rim. Put the crust in the freezer for 15 minutes.

Remove the crust from the freezer and spread the mousse over the bottom. Arrange the strawberries on top of the mousse. Refrigerate for at least 1 hour before serving. Serve chilled or at room temperature. Covered with plastic wrap and stored in the refrigerator, Chocolate Pie or Tart with Strawberries will keep for 3 days.

CHOCOLATE PIE OR TART WITH RASPBERRIES: Replace the strawberries with 2 cups of fresh raspberries.

Per serving: calories: 460, protein: 11 g, fat: 28 g, carbohydrate: 45 g, fiber: 14 g, sodium: 77 mg

MOUSSES, PUDDINGS, AND SWEET SAUCES

The versatile recipes in this section make creating gourmet treats quick and easy. Sweet sauces can garnish many desserts. Try Vanilla Crème Sauce (page 185) on Apple Crisp (page 171) and Raspberry Sauce (page 186) on Flourless Chocolate Cake (page 162). Puddings and mousses can be eaten straight or used to fill pies and tarts. For example, if you have Chocolate Mousse (page 180) on hand, you can make a Chocolate Pie or Tart with Strawberries (page 177) in ten minutes. Or pair mousses, puddings, and sweet sauces with fresh fruit to create a parfait. In a small wine glass, layer one or two mousses, puddings, or sweet sauces with sliced fresh fruits and berries of different colors, such as bananas, blackberries, kiwifruit, mangoes, pineapple, and strawberries. Continue to layer until the glass is full. Try Key Lime Mousse (page 179) with Mango Pudding (page 183) and blackberries and banana slices or Chocolate Mousse (page 180) with Vanilla Crème Sauce (page 185) and raspberries.

You need only three ingredients for this luscious, bright green mousse.

key lime mousse

YIELD: 1 CUP, 3 SERVINGS

¾ **cup mashed avocados** (1½ avocados)

¼ **cup agave nectar or maple syrup**

2 **tablespoons freshly squeezed lime juice**

Sliced kiwifruit or fresh berries or a combination,
   for garnish

EQUIPMENT

small bowl

fork

measuring cups

citrus juicer or reamer

measuring spoons

food processor

rubber spatula

cutting board

paring knife

Put the avocados, agave nectar, and lime juice in a food processor fitted with the S blade and process until smooth, stopping occasionally to scrape down the work bowl with a rubber spatula. Garnish with kiwifruit. Serve immediately.

NOTE: To make a double batch, increase the amounts to 1½ cups of mashed avocados (3 avocados), ½ cup of agave nectar, and ¼ cup of freshly squeezed lime juice. Yield: 2 cups, 4 servings.

KEY LIME SHERBET: Put the Key Lime Mousse in the freezer for at least 4 hours. Thaw for 15 minutes before serving.

LEMON MOUSSE: Replace the lime juice with 2 tablespoons of freshly squeezed lemon juice.

Per serving: calories: 227, protein: 2 g, fat: 13 g, carbohydrate: 24 g, fiber: 7 g, sodium: 7 mg

No one will know that avocado replaces butter, cream, and eggs in this silky treat.

chocolate mousse

SEE PHOTO FACING PAGE 185.

YIELD: 1 CUP, 3 SERVINGS

¼ cup pitted medjool dates, soaked in water for 10 minutes and drained

¼ cup maple syrup or agave nectar

½ teaspoon vanilla extract (optional)

¾ cup mashed avocados (1½ avocados)

6 tablespoons unsweetened cocoa or carob powder

¼ cup water

EQUIPMENT

small bowls, two

small colander or fine-mesh strainer

measuring cups

measuring spoons

food processor

fork

rubber spatula

Put the dates, maple syrup, and optional vanilla extract in a food processor fitted with the S blade and process until smooth. Add the avocados and cocoa powder and process until creamy, stopping occasionally to scrape down the work bowl with a rubber spatula. Add the water and process briefly. Stored in a sealed container, Chocolate Mousse will keep for 3 days in the refrigerator or 2 weeks in the freezer. Serve chilled or at room temperature.

NOTE: To make a double batch, increase the amounts to ½ cup of pitted medjool dates, soaked, ½ cup of maple syrup, 1 teaspoon of vanilla extract, 1½ cups of mashed avocados (3 avocados), ¾ cup of cocoa or carob powder, and ½ cup of water. Yield: 2 cups, 4 servings.

CHOCOLATE BUTTERCREAM FROSTING: Omit the water.

CHOCOLATE ICE CREAM: Put the Chocolate Mousse in the freezer for at least 4 hours. Thaw for 15 minutes before serving. Stored in a sealed container, Chocolate Ice Cream will keep for 1 month in the freezer.

CHOCOLATE SAUCE: Increase the water to ½ cup for a small batch and 1 cup for a double batch.

Per serving: calories: 281, protein: 4 g, fat: 15 g, carbohydrate: 32 g, fiber: 11 g, sodium: 12 mg

This pudding tastes like the old-fashioned kind, with graham crumble, creamy custard, and banana slices.

banana pudding

YIELD: 3 SERVINGS

½ cup **Vanilla Crème Sauce** (page 185)
1 banana, cut in half
¼ cup **Crumble Topping** (page 168)

EQUIPMENT

measuring cups

blender

cutting board

paring knife

measuring spoons

rubber spatula

small bowl

Put the sauce and half of the banana in a blender and process on medium speed until smooth. Thinly slice the other banana half. Put 2 tablespoons of the topping in a small bowl. Add the following in layers: half of the banana slices, ¼ cup of the banana mixture, the rest of the banana slices, and the remaining banana mixture. Top with the remaining 2 tablespoons of topping. Serve immediately.

Per serving: calories: 297, protein: 7 g, fat: 20 g, carbohydrate: 25 g, fiber: 3 g, sodium: 29 mg

Comforts like chocolate—without caffeine or sugar. Try this nutritious pudding for dessert, a snack, or even breakfast.

carob pudding

YIELD: 1 CUP, 2 SERVINGS

2 bananas, broken into 2 or 3 pieces

2 tablespoons raw tahini

¼ cup carob powder

EQUIPMENT

measuring spoons

measuring cups

food processor

rubber spatula

Put all the ingredients in a food processor fitted with the S-blade and process until smooth, stopping occasionally to scrape down the work bowl with a rubber spatula. Stored in a sealed container in the refrigerator, Carob Pudding will keep for 3 days.

Per serving: calories: 242, protein: 4 g, fat: 8 g, carbohydrate: 39 g, fiber: 7 g, sodium: 14 mg

Don't let the simple ingredient list fool you—this fat-free pudding is rich and creamy.

mango pudding

YIELD: 1 CUP, 3 SERVINGS

1½ **cups fresh or thawed frozen mango chunks**

½ **cup chopped dried mangoes** (cut into pieces with kitchen shears)**, soaked in water for 10 minutes and drained**

¼ **cup sliced kiwifruit, fresh blueberries, or fresh blackberries** (optional)

EQUIPMENT

measuring cups

kitchen shears

small bowl

small colander or fine-mesh strainer

blender

rubber spatula

Put the fresh and dried mangoes in a blender and process on high speed until smooth. Transfer to a serving bowl and top with the kiwifruit just before serving if desired. Stored in a sealed container in the refrigerator, Mango Pudding will keep for 3 days. Serve chilled or at room temperature.

NOTE: To make a double batch, increase the amounts to 3 cups of mango chunks and 1 cup of chopped dried mangoes, soaked. Yield: 2 cups, 4 servings.

PINEAPPLE PUDDING: Replace the fresh and dried mangoes with 1½ cups of fresh or thawed frozen pineapple and ½ cup of dried pineapple.

Per serving: calories: 220, protein: 3 g, fat: 0 g, carbohydrate: 55 g, fiber: 5 g, sodium 1 mg

The perfect frosting for Walnut-Raisin Cake (page 159).

lemon glaze

YIELD: ½ CUP, 4 SERVINGS

½ cup pitted medjool dates, soaked in water
for 10 minutes and drained

2 tablespoons freshly squeezed lemon juice

2 tablespoons water

EQUIPMENT

measuring cups

small bowl

small colander or fine-mesh strainer

citrus juicer or reamer

measuring spoons

food processor

rubber spatula

Put the dates, lemon juice, and water in a food processor fitted with the S blade and process until smooth, stopping occasionally to scrape down the work bowl with a rubber spatula. Stored in a sealed container in the refrigerator, Lemon Glaze will keep for 5 days.

NOTE: For a double batch, increase the amounts to 1 cup of pitted medjool dates, soaked, ¼ cup of freshly squeezed lemon juice, and ¼ cup of water. Yield: 1 cup, 8 servings.

ORANGE GLAZE: Replace the lemon juice and water with ¼ cup of freshly squeezed orange juice for a small batch and ½ cup for a double batch.

Per serving: calories: 63, protein: 0 g, fat: 0 g, carbohydrate: 15 g, fiber: 2 g, sodium: 1 mg

Almond Cookies, *page 164*

Blackberry Crisp, *page 172*, **with Vanilla Ice Cream,** *page 191*

Flourless Chocolate Cake, *page 162,*
with Raspberry Sauce, *page 186*

parfait of Chocolate Mousse, *page 180,*
and Vanilla Crème Sauce, *page 185*

Serve with Tropical Fruit Salad (page 32) for an elegant breakfast or brunch.

sweet orange cream sauce

SEE PHOTO FACING PAGE 25.

YIELD: 1½ CUPS, 6 SERVINGS

1 cup soaked cashews (see page 7)

¾ cup freshly squeezed orange juice

2 tablespoons agave nectar or maple syrup

EQUIPMENT

measuring cups

citrus juicer or reamer

measuring spoons

blender

rubber spatula

Put all the ingredients in a blender and process on high speed until smooth. Cover and refrigerate for at least 30 minutes before serving. Stored in a sealed container in the refrigerator, Sweet Orange Cream Sauce will keep for 3 days.

SWEET LEMON CREAM SAUCE: Replace the orange juice with ¼ cup of freshly squeezed lemon juice and add ½ cup of water.

Per serving: calories: 174, protein: 5 g, fat: 11 g, carbohydrate: 15 g, fiber: 1 g, sodium: 3 mg

Serve this delicious sauce instead of whipped cream with fresh berries, cakes, crisps, pies, or tarts.

vanilla crème sauce

SEE PHOTO ON FACING PAGE.

YIELD: 1 CUP, 8 SERVINGS

1 cup soaked cashews (see page 7)

¼ cup plus 2 tablespoons water

2 tablespoons maple syrup or agave nectar

1 teaspoon vanilla extract

EQUIPMENT

measuring cups

measuring spoons

blender

rubber spatula

Put all the ingredients in a blender and process on high speed until smooth. Cover and refrigerate for at least 30 minutes before serving. Stored in a sealed container in the refrigerator, Vanilla Crème Sauce will keep for 5 days.

Per serving: calories: 120, protein: 3 g, fat: 8 g, carbohydrate: 9 g, fiber: 1 g, sodium: 3 mg

The classic accompaniment to Flourless Chocolate Cake (page 162).

raspberry sauce

SEE PHOTO FACING PAGE 185.

YIELD: 1 CUP, 8 SERVINGS

8 ounces frozen raspberries, thawed and drained (1 cup)

¼ cup pitted medjool dates, soaked in water for 10 minutes and drained

EQUIPMENT

measuring cups

small colander or fine-mesh strainer

small bowl

blender

rubber spatula

Put all the ingredients in a blender and process on medium speed until smooth. Stored in a sealed container in the refrigerator, Raspberry Sauce will keep for 3 days.

BLACKBERRY, BLUEBERRY, OR CHERRY SAUCE: Replace the raspberries with 8 ounces frozen blackberries, blueberries, or pitted cherries, thawed and drained (1 cup).

Per serving: calories: 30, protein: 0 g, fat: 0 g, carbohydrate: 5 g, fiber: 2 g, sodium: 0 mg

SHAKES, ICE CREAMS, AND SORBETS

If you love milkshakes and ice cream, try my Banana Shake (page 188), Banana Ice Cream (page 190), or a sorbet. Unlike heavy dairy-based versions, these frozen treats will leave you energized.

Satisfies that milkshake craving.

banana shake

YIELD: 1½ CUPS, 1 SERVING

1 frozen banana (see page 15), **thawed for 5 minutes and broken into 2 or 3 pieces**

½ **cup Almond Milk** (page 58)

1½ **teaspoons maple syrup or agave nectar**

½ **teaspoon vanilla extract**

EQUIPMENT

measuring cups

measuring spoons

blender

rubber spatula

Put all the ingredients in a blender. Process on medium speed until smooth and creamy. Serve immediately.

STRAWBERRY SHAKE: Omit the vanilla extract and add 1 cup of fresh or frozen strawberries. Yield: 2 cups, 2 servings.

Per serving: calories: 257, protein: 5 g, fat: 10 g, carbohydrate: 37 g, fiber: 6 g, sodium: 3 mg

Maca, a root from the Andes, lends a pleasant, malty taste to this frosty shake.

chocolate malt

YIELD: 2 CUPS, 2 SERVINGS

2 frozen bananas (see page 15)**, thawed for 5 minutes and broken into 2 or 3 pieces**

1 cup Hemp Milk (page 57)

3 tablespoons unsweetened cocoa or carob powder

1 tablespoon maca powder (see Glossary, page 200; optional)

EQUIPMENT

measuring cups

measuring spoons

blender

rubber spatula

Put all of the ingredients in a blender. Process on high speed until smooth and creamy. Serve immediately.

Per serving: calories: 279, protein: 14 g, fat: 11 g, carbohydrate: 33 g, fiber: 7 g, sodium: 13 mg

This dairy-free ice cream is so rich, you'll go bananas.

banana ice cream

YIELD: 2 CUPS, 2 SERVINGS

3 very ripe bananas, cut into ½-inch slices

EQUIPMENT

cutting board

chef's knife

plate

food processor

rubber spatula

Put the banana slices on a plate and put in the freezer for 4 to 12 hours. Put the frozen banana slices in a food processor fitted with the S blade and process until smooth, about 3 minutes. Let the machine run until the bananas are completely smooth and creamy. Serve immediately.

STRAWBERRY-BANANA ICE CREAM: Omit one of the bananas. Add 1 cup of frozen strawberries to the food processor along with the frozen banana slices.

Per serving: calories: 152, protein: 2 g, fat: 1 g, carbohydrate: 35 g, fiber: 4 g, sodium: 2 mg

This easy ice cream tastes so rich and creamy, you won't believe it's dairy-free. It makes purchasing an ice-cream maker worthwhile!

vanilla ice cream

SEE PHOTO FACING PAGE 184.

YIELD: 1½ CUPS, 2 SERVINGS

1½ cups Almond Cream (page 58) or Cashew Cream (page 60)

2 tablespoons maple syrup or agave nectar

½ teaspoon vanilla extract

Dash salt

EQUIPMENT

measuring cups

measuring spoons

medium bowl

whisk

ice-cream maker

Put all the ingredients in a medium bowl and whisk to combine. Freeze in an ice-cream maker according to the manufacturer's directions. Serve immediately.

Per serving: calories: 283, protein: 8 g, fat: 18 g, carbohydrate: 27 g, fiber: 5 g, sodium: 56 mg

Fat- and sugar-free, raw sorbets are the ultimate guilt-free dessert.

mango sorbet

YIELD: 1 SERVING

1½ cups frozen mango chunks, thawed for 5 minutes

EQUIPMENT
measuring cups
food processor
rubber spatula

Put the mango chunks in a food processor fitted with the S blade and process until smooth, stopping occasionally to scrape down the work bowl with a rubber spatula. Serve immediately.

CHERRY SORBET: Replace the mango chunks with 1½ cups of frozen pitted cherries.

Per serving: calories: 161, protein: 1 g, fat: 1 g, carbohydrate: 38 g, fiber: 4 g, sodium: 5 mg

NEXT STEPS

ow that you've reached the end of *Raw Food Made Easy for 1 or 2 People*, I hope you will consider this book as a starting gate not a finish line. There's a wide, wonderful world of raw food and its enthusiasts out there for you. And the Internet makes it easier than ever to keep up with new ideas, expand your knowledge, and connect with other people who share your interest. I continually update my website, learnrawfood.com, so we can share ideas, recipes, tips, and videos.

As an instructor at Living Light Culinary Institute in California and at other locations around the country, I enjoy meeting people and demonstrating raw-food preparation in person. But since everyone can't make a trip to the West Coast or get to one of my local classes, I've created a fun, friendly, online training called *Ready for Raw* that allows you to learn with me from your own living room or kitchen. In fifteen easy-to-follow interactive sessions, I expand on the concepts in *Raw Food Made Easy for 1 or 2 People* to provide a deeper, broader foundation in raw-food preparation. You can make recipes right along with me, following step-by-step as I prepare my latest dishes. At under $15 per session, it's a good value. If an online course appeals to you, please go to my site, where you can sample a session for free.

Food is a pleasure we can all share. Luciano Pavarotti famously said, "One of the very nicest things about life is the way we must regularly stop whatever it is we are doing and devote our attention to eating."

For now, let's not say good-bye. Just "until we meet again."

GLOSSARY

Cooking Terms

DICE. To dice is to cut food into very small cubes, about ¼ inch.

JULIENNE. To julienne is to cut food into matchstick strips.

MARINATE. To marinate is to flavor and tenderize ingredients by letting them stand in a dressing of oil, acid (such as citrus juice), and salt.

MINCE. To mince is to chop food into very fine pieces. Ingredients that are most commonly minced include onions, celery, garlic, ginger, and fresh herbs.

Equipment

BAMBOO SUSHI MAT. A woven bamboo sushi mat is essential for making tight, professional-quality nori rolls.

BLENDER. A blender is an electric appliance that processes ingredients until they are smooth or liquefied. I recommend the two-speed Oster Classic Beehive with glass container, the KitchenAid KSB560, and the Tribest Personal Blender for travel or single-serving smoothies. You may also wish to invest in a powerful high-speed model, such as a Vitamix or Blendtec.

CHEF'S KNIFE. A seven- to ten-inch knife with a broad blade and very sharp edge, a chef's knife is designed for slicing, dicing, chopping, and mincing. I recommend an eight-inch knife for most tasks—either a European-style or a santoku Asian-style knife, depending on personal preference. My favorite brands are Henckels, Wüsthof, and Mac. Kyocera ceramic knives are ideal for cutting fruit and lettuce, since they will not alter the delicate taste or color of these foods. For travel, I recommend a small knife with a sheath, such as the 3.5-inch Messermeister Picnic Knife.

CITRUS JUICER OR REAMER. A wide cone with ridges, a juicer or reamer crushes the inside of halved citrus fruit, releasing the juice. Some models come with a dish to catch the juice; others are handheld. I recommend models that use interchangeable cones to accommodate the different sizes of limes, oranges, and grapefruits, such as the Oxo Good Grips Citrus Juicer. Electric juicers are efficient when you want to make larger quantities.

COFFEE GRINDER. A coffee grinder is an electric appliance useful for grinding seeds, such as flax, hemp, sesame, and sunflower.

CUTTING BOARD. A cutting board is a surface, preferably made from wood or bamboo, for cutting fruits and vegetables. For travel, I recommend Progressive Flexible Chopping Mats.

DEHYDRATOR. An electric appliance for drying food indoors, a dehydrator is used to make dried fruits and vegetables, seasoned nuts and seeds, fruit leathers, and raw breads, crackers, cookies, and bars. I recommend the Excalibur five- or nine-tray model, with Paraflexx sheets (which are essential if you will be drying wet mixtures, such as fruit leather and cracker batters).

FOOD PROCESSOR. An electric appliance with interchangeable blades and cutting disks and a removable bowl and lid, a food processor is used for chopping, grinding, puréeing, slicing, and shredding ingredients. I recommend the Cuisinart seven-, eleven-, and fourteen-cup capacity models. A seven-cup machine is fine for regular home use, but if you plan to prepare food for large numbers of people, a fourteen-cup machine is essential. At under $100, the Hamilton Beach fourteen-cup food processor is an excellent value.

GARLIC PRESS. A garlic press is a handheld device used to crush garlic cloves by forcing them through a grid of small holes. I recommend the Zyliss brand.

GRATER. A grater is a utensil with sharp-edged holes against which vegetables are rubbed in order to shred them. A file grater has especially tiny, razor-like edges, ideal for removing the zest from citrus fruits and for grating ginger, nutmeg, and chocolate. I recommend the Microplane brand.

HONING STEEL. A honing steel is a long rod that realigns the edges of knives to keep them sharp. To hone, draw your knife at a 20-degree angle, from base to tip, along the steel. Repeat several times on each side of the blade. If you do this every time you use a knife, you won't have to sharpen it for months.

ICE-CREAM MAKER. An ice-cream maker is a manual or electric appliance that produces ice cream by rotating a canister around a paddle. The canister, which holds a freezing agent, must be kept in the freezer for at least several hours before using. I recommend the 1½-quart Cuisinart automatic ice-cream maker, which costs about $55.

JUICER. A juicer is an electric appliance that extracts juice from fruits and vegetables. A slow-speed, low-temperature model is best, since it produces the maximum yield and preserves nutrients and enzymes. I recommend Tribest juicers (Solostar or Green Star models). Though not ideal for dark leafy greens, such as kale, the Breville juicer is also a good option, as it is easy to use and relatively inexpensive. It works well for making apple, beet, carrot, celery, and cucumber juices.

KITCHEN SHEARS. High-quality kitchen shears are perfect for cutting broccoli florets, snipping kale into thin strips, and opening plastic packaging.

KNIFE BLOCK. A wooden block with slits designed for knife storage, a knife block is kept on the counter so knives are readily available, organized, and protected. You can also purchase an in-drawer knife holder to save counter space.

KNIFE SHARPENER. There are two types of knife sharpeners: natural stone and commercial. Before using a sharpening stone, first read the instructions to determine if yours needs to be soaked in water or mineral oil, then draw the knife toward you across the stone at a 20-degree angle several times, from base to tip. Repeat on the other side of the blade. With a commercial knife sharpener (I recommend Chef's Choice manual sharpener or a sharpener that is designed for your particular brand of knives), refer to the instruction booklet that comes with it. Serrated, ceramic, and very fine knives should be sharpened professionally.

MANDOLINE. A mandoline is a manual tool with various blades for slicing and julienning fruits and vegetables uniformly. I recommend the Oxo Good Grips Mandoline and the Borner V slicer. A ceramic option, made by Kyocera, is similar to a mandoline, but its blade stays sharp longer than steel and will not alter the taste or color of foods. It does not have multiple blades for different thicknesses but is ideal for cutting paper-thin slices of cucumber or onion.

MASON JARS. Mason jars are glass containers useful for storing staple ingredients, salad dressings, and sauces; for soaking nuts and seeds; for shaking green powders and ground flaxseeds into juice; for transporting drinks and soups; and for growing sprouts. I recommend pint- and quart-sized jars with widemouthed openings and metal screw-top lids.

MESH BAG. Also called a sprout bag or nut milk bag, a mesh bag is more effective than a strainer for extracting milk from blended nut mixtures.

RAMEKIN. A ceramic dish three inches in diameter, a ramekin holds about six ounces. It is ideal for individual servings of crisps, mousses, and puddings.

S BLADE. The S blade of a food processor is used for chopping, grinding, and puréeing.

SALAD SPINNER. A salad spinner is for washing and spin-drying salad greens as dry as possible.

SERRATED KNIFE, FIVE-INCH. Small, razor-sharp, and maneuverable, a five-inch serrated knife is ideal for cutting tomatoes, removing the peel from citrus fruits, and slicing soft fruits, such as kiwifruit, peaches, and plums.

SPATULA. A versatile utensil available in a variety of shapes and sizes, a spatula is made from rubber or metal. Rubber models with sturdy, flexible heads are best for mixing and removing mixtures from a food processor. Rubber models with narrow heads are useful for removing mixtures from the bottom of a blender. Metal spatulas with flexible, narrow heads are ideal for frosting cakes, while models with wide, offset heads are essential for lifting slices of cake or pie from the pan. Use a square-headed one for serving lasagne, brownies, and square-shaped pieces of cake and a triangular one for serving pies and tarts.

TART PAN. With straight sides and fluted edges, tart pans come in a variety of sizes, ranging from four to twelve inches in diameter. I recommend nine-inch pans for full-sized tarts and five-inch for individual tarts. Buy a pan with a removable bottom, so that the outer ring can be released while keeping the crust intact.

VEGETABLE SPIRAL SLICER. Also called a garnishing machine, a vegetable spiral slicer transforms zucchini and other vegetables into delicate angel-hair pasta.

VITAMIX. A Vitamix is a high-speed, high-performance blender that makes smoothies, nut milks, sauces, and soups in seconds.

Food Terms and Ingredients

AGAVE NECTAR. A natural sweetener made from the juice of the agave plant, agave nectar is 90 percent fructose and has a lower glycemic index than cane sugar, honey, or maple syrup. Choose light agave nectar for mild sweetness, and dark agave nectar for a deep, molasses-like flavor.

ALMOND BUTTER, RAW. A spread made from ground raw almonds, almond butter can replace peanut butter, which is made from roasted nuts.

ALOE VERA JUICE. Extracted from the leaves of the aloe vera plant, aloe vera juice has been used for centuries for its soothing and healing properties. Look for whole-leaf, preservative-free juice.

ANTIOXIDANTS. Found in fruits and vegetables, antioxidants are nutrients, including vitamins A and C, that neutralize free-radical molecules, which can contribute to cancer and other diseases.

ARAME. A species of kelp, arame is a well-known sea vegetable used in Japanese cuisine. It has a mild, semisweet flavor. Soak in water for five minutes and drain before serving.

ARUGULA. A salad green with a peppery, slightly bitter flavor, arugula is also known as rocket.

BALSAMIC VINEGAR. An Italian vinegar made from grape juice, balsamic vinegar has a deep sweet-and-sour flavor. True balsamic vinegar (*aceto balsamic tradizionale*) is aged for a minimum of ten years in wooden casks. The finest and most expensive vinegars are aged for twenty-five to fifty years.

BETA-CAROTENE. Found in green, orange, and red vegetables, beta-carotene is a nutrient that the body converts into vitamin A.

BLACK MISSION FIGS. Purple-black in color, black Mission figs have a deep, complex flavor.

BLUE-GREEN ALGAE. Blue-green algae is an excellent source of beta-carotene, chlorophyll, protein, and trace minerals. The three main types are chlorella, Klamath Lake algae, and spirulina.

BRAGG LIQUID AMINOS. A seasoning made from soybeans and distilled water, Bragg Liquid Aminos is less salty than tamari.

BRAZIL NUTS. Rich and creamy, Brazil nuts are a concentrated source of the mineral selenium.

CALIMYRNA FIGS. Golden in color, calimyrna figs have a honey-like flavor.

CAPERS. Capers are pickled flower buds that are used in condiments and sauces.

CAROB POWDER. A dark brown powder made from ground carob seeds and pods, carob powder tastes similar to cocoa powder but has no caffeine and is naturally sweet. It is available raw or roasted.

CHIA SEEDS. Tiny chia seeds are an excellent source of omega-3 fatty acids, fiber, protein, and minerals.

CIDER VINEGAR, RAW. Cider vinegar is a fruity vinegar made from apple juice. I recommend the raw, unpasteurized kind, which contains beneficial bacteria and enzymes.

COCOA POWDER, UNSWEETENED. Unsweetened cocoa powder is made from raw or roasted cacao beans that have been processed to extract the cacao butter, then dried and ground. Use a naturally processed, organic brand, such as Green and Black's (roasted) or Navitas Naturals (raw).

COCONUT NECTAR AND SUGAR. Coconut nectar is a low-glycemic and mineral-rich sweetener. With a caramel-like flavor, it is stronger tasting than agave nectar but can replace agave nectar in many recipes. Coconut sugar can be used as an alternative to cane sugar or maple sugar.

COCONUT OIL, EXTRA-VIRGIN. A naturally saturated fat, coconut oil is made up of medium-chain fatty acids, which are thought to increase metabolism and promote weight loss.

CREMINI MUSHROOMS. Cremini mushrooms are small, immature portobello mushrooms and are more flavorful than the common white button variety.

DULSE. A reddish-purple sea vegetable with a soft texture and salty taste, dulse is high in iron and trace minerals. Available in flakes and whole-leaf form, it needs no soaking.

ESSENTIAL FATTY ACIDS. Providing important nutrients for growth, energy, and healthy skin and hair, essential fatty acids are not produced by the body and must be obtained from food. Rich sources include walnuts and seeds, such as flaxseeds and chia seeds. Refined oils, heated oils, hydrogenated oils, and saturated fats lack essential fatty acids.

EXTRA-VIRGIN OLIVE OIL. A delicious, fruity oil, extra-virgin olive oil is the product of the first pressing of tree-ripened olives. It is extracted using a low-temperature and chemical-free process that involves only mechanical pressure. Extra-virgin olive oil is rich in healthful monounsaturated fats.

FILTERED WATER. Filtered water has been run through a carbon block to remove chlorine, other chemicals, and heavy metals, such as lead and mercury.

FLAXSEED OIL. A nutritious oil rich in omega-3 fatty acids, flaxseed oil is very fragile and should never be heated. Store it in the refrigerator or freezer.

FLAXSEEDS. Flaxseeds are tiny brown or golden seeds that are an excellent source of omega-3 fatty acids and fiber. To preserve their delicate oils, flaxseeds should be consumed raw. Grind them in a coffee grinder before using.

FRISÉE. A salad green with a mildly bitter flavor and feathery texture, frisée is often used in mesclun mixes. If unavailable, curly endive is a suitable substitution.

GLYCEMIC INDEX. The glycemic index is a measuring system that ranks foods according to how much they raise blood sugar levels.

GOJI BERRIES. Goji berries are one of nature's most nutritionally dense fruits. A rich source of complete protein, vitamin C, and trace minerals, goji berries are delicious whether eaten straight or soaked before adding to fruit smoothies and cereals.

GREEN POWDERS. Green powders are nutritious whole-food supplements made from dehydrated wheat, Kamut, and barley grasses; blue-green algae; and dehydrated green leafy vegetables. There are many good brands available; one of my favorites is Vitamineral Green.

HEMPSEEDS. Tiny, mild-flavored hempseeds are a concentrated source of complete protein and omega-3 fatty acids. I recommend grinding them in a coffee grinder and adding them to juices and smoothies.

HYDROGENATED OILS. Hydrogenated oils are unhealthful vegetable oils that have been hardened by heating at very high temperatures. This process destroys the essential fatty acids in the oil and replaces them with harmful trans-fatty acids.

KALE. A cruciferous vegetable with dark green, wrinkled leaves, kale is available in several varieties, including curly green and red kale and dinosaur (or lacinato) kale.

I prefer dinosaur kale, since its flatter leaves are easier to cut into thin strips for salads and to feed into juicers for green drinks.

MACA POWDER. Made from the maca root, which is native to Peru, maca powder is used as both a root vegetable and a medicinal herb. Add a tablespoon to a raw smoothie or shake for a sweet taste similar to malt.

MAPLE SUGAR. Maple sugar is created when the sap of the sugar maple tree is boiled for longer than is needed to create maple syrup. It can be used to replace whole cane sugar in many recipes.

MEDJOOL DATES. Nicknamed "nature's candy," the medjool is an intensely sweet and sticky date that features an amber color, wrinkled skin, and chewy texture. Always use soft dates for processing in raw-food recipes. Pit the dates yourself; they are fresher than prepitted. Stored in an airtight container in the refrigerator, medjool dates will keep for six months.

MESCLUN. Mesclun is a mixture of young salad greens, which often includes arugula, baby romaine lettuce, baby red leaf and oak leaf lettuces, frisée, mâche, and radicchio. Choose greens with crisp leaves and no signs of wilting. Refrigerate in a plastic bag for up to five days, and wash and spin-dry just before using.

MISO. A paste made from fermented soybeans and salt, miso is rich in enzymes and healthful bacteria. Buy unpasteurized miso, which is available in the refrigerated section of most natural food stores. I recommend mellow white miso, which is sweet and mild and lends a rich flavor to soups and sauces.

NORI SHEETS. Thin, dried sheets of the sea vegetable nori are used to wrap sushi. They are available raw or toasted.

PARFAIT. A parfait is a layered dessert made from ice cream or mousse, fruit, and a dessert sauce or whipped cream. Parfaits are traditionally served in tall, narrow dessert or wine glasses.

PÂTÉ. A finely ground spread or filling, pâté is well seasoned with garlic or onions, herbs, and salt. Raw pâtés are made from nuts, seeds, and vegetables.

PHYTONUTRIENTS. Natural compounds found in plant-based foods, phytonutrients are thought to enhance the immune system, slow the aging process, and help prevent heart disease and cancer. Common phytonutrients include bioflavonoids, carotenoids, chlorophyll, and lycopene.

PORTOBELLO MUSHROOMS. Portobello mushrooms are large cremini mushrooms with a meaty texture. Stuff them with any pâté or dip for an instant entrée.

PROTEIN POWDER, RAW VEGAN. A refined supplement used to boost protein intake, raw vegan protein powders may be made from soy, brown rice, peas, or hempseeds. I recommend raw organic hemp protein powder.

PUMPKIN SEEDS. Pumpkin seeds, also known as pepitas, have a light green color and a delicate, nutty taste. They are a good source of magnesium and zinc and are thought to promote prostate health.

RADICCHIO. Radicchio is a peppery, bitter, and crunchy salad green with red and white leaves and a tight head.

RAW FOOD. Raw food is unprocessed, unrefined, and untreated with heat.

RAW OLIVES. Raw olives are naturally cured and sun-dried at low temperatures, without chemicals.

RICE PAPER. Round spring roll wrappers made from rice flour, rice paper is available in dried form and must be softened in water before using.

ROMAINE HEARTS. Romaine lettuce heads that have been trimmed down to the succulent inner leaves, romaine hearts are typically sold in packs of three.

SALT, UNREFINED. Unrefined salt is sun-dried so that its natural mineral content is intact. I recommend Celtic Sea Salt and Himalayan Crystal Salt.

SATURATED FAT. A type of fat that is solid at room temperature, saturated fat is found in its highest concentrations in high-fat dairy products, red meats, coconut oil, cocoa butter, palm kernel oil, and palm oil. Saturated fats are more heat-stable than other oils, so if you sauté foods, I recommend using coconut oil. Olive oil has some saturated fat in addition to monounsaturated fat and is stable for sautéing at lower temperatures.

SESAME OIL, COLD-PRESSED. Cold-pressed sesame oil is made from raw (unroasted) seeds. Its nutty flavor complements Asian-themed dishes. Toasted sesame oil, while not raw, makes a delicious garnish when drizzled in small amounts on soups and salads.

SESAME SEEDS, UNHULLED. Unhulled, brown sesame seeds have more calcium than hulled, white sesame seeds.

SHALLOTS. Tiny, delicately flavored onions, shallots are often used in French cooking, especially in salad dressings and sauces.

SHIITAKE MUSHROOMS, DRIED. Dried shiitake mushrooms have an intense, earthy flavor. Soak in water for about 30 minutes to reconstitute.

SHOYU. A salty seasoning made from fermented soybeans and wheat, shoyu is commonly called soy sauce.

SPRING WATER. Mineral-rich spring water is pumped from natural springs in the earth. There are many excellent brands; I enjoy Fiji Water.

SPROUTS. Sprouts are grains, legumes, nuts, or seeds that have been soaked, drained, and left to germinate. Sprouts are rich in amino acids, phytonutrients, vitamins, minerals, and protein.

STEVIA. A naturally sweet South American herb that contains no calories or carbohydrates, stevia will not raise blood sugar levels.

SUN-DRIED TOMATOES. Plum tomatoes that have been dried at low temperatures to a chewy texture and tart-sweet taste, sun-dried tomatoes are available oil-packed or dry. Dry tomatoes must be soaked for thirty minutes before using.

TAHINI, RAW. Tahini is a creamy paste made from raw, hulled sesame seeds.

TAMARI. A traditional Japanese soy sauce made without wheat, tamari has a rich, salty, wine-like flavor.

TRANS FATS. Trans-fatty acids (or trans fats) are created when vegetable oils are hydrogenated, refined, or heated at high temperatures, or go rancid because of overexposure to air and light. Many breads, cookies, crackers, and snack foods contain these unnatural fats. Trans fats compete with essential fatty acids for absorption, creating metabolic imbalances and deposits in the arteries.

WAKAME. Wakame is a sea vegetable that turns bright green when soaked and looks like spinach. It's rich in magnesium and fiber. Soak for ten minutes and drain before serving.

WATERCRESS. A crisp, leafy salad green with a slightly bitter, peppery flavor, watercress is sold in small bunches.

WHOLE CANE SUGAR. Whole cane sugar is naturally squeezed, dried, and ground sugarcane juice. I recommend Rapunzel brand. If unavailable, organic Sucanat or maple sugar are suitable substitutions.

WHOLE OAT GROATS. Whole groats are oats that have not been flattened into the more-familiar rolled oats. They contain more fiber and nutrients than rolled oats. Look for groats that are untreated with heat (manufacturers sometimes steam them to extend shelf life).

ZEST. The outermost skin layer of citrus fruit, zest is removed with a zester, peeler, or file grater. Remove only the colored portion of the peel, not the bitter white pith beneath.

INDEX

Recipe titles appear in *italics*.

A

agave nectar, 197
Alfredo, Zucchini Fettuccine, 139
algae, blue-green, 198
almond(s)
  butter, 197
    Cookies, Not Peanut Butter, 163
    as pantry item, 155
    recipe for, 78
    in sandwiches, 131
    Sauce, Mock Peanut, 75
  Cream, 58
    Berries and, 30
  in desserts
    Cake, Spanish Fig, 161
    Cookies, Almond, 164
    Cookies, Not Peanut Butter, 163
    Crust, Almond, 169
  Flour, 165
  in granola, 53
  Milk, 58
    Chocolate, 58
    with Stevia, 58
    straining, 12
  in muesli recipe, 55
  as pantry item, 155
  in pâté, 71
  in salad, 102
  as snacks, 61, 156
  soaking, 7, 13
  and Sunflower Seed Cereal, 52
Aloe Juice, 21
aloe vera juice, 197
Aminos, Bragg Liquid, 198
antioxidants, 197
appetizer(s)
  California Rolls as, 134
  dips and pâtés as, 66
  leftover green smoothie as, 38
  Stuffed Dates in Marinara Sauce as, 140

Stuffed Mushroom, 138
apple(s)
  cutting, 11, 104
  in desserts
    Crisp, 171
    Crumb Cake, 160
    Pie or Tart, 175
  in green smoothies, 40
    Apple-Banana, 39
    Fall, 49
    Frosty Banana-Apple, 43
    Garden Vegetable, 50
    Peachy Apple, 44
  in juices
    Fasting, 22
    Pink Apple, 19
    Super Green, 24
    Sweet Green, 23
  in salads
    Harvest, 105
    Thai, 104
  Sandwiches, 131
  -sauce, 33
  as snacks, 61
    nut butters for, 15
  Soup, Spinach-, 89
  storing, 8
  Vinaigrette, 113
  when traveling, 155
appliances, electric, 4, 12–13
apricots, dried
  in fruit compote, 30
  as snacks, 61
  soaking, 7
arame, 197
Arame Salad, 106
arugula (rocket), 110, 197
Asian Greens, 151
Asian salad, 106
asparagus, steamed, 65
avocado(s)
  Boat, 136
  creaminess of, in salad dressings, 112
  cutting, 11
  in dessert(s), 157
    fillings, 167
    Mousse, Chocolate, 180

Mousse, Key Lime, 179
in entrées
  California Rolls, 134
  Garden Wrap, 133
  Lasagne, 135
Fruit Salad, 31
in guacamole, 67
-Lime Dressing, 115
Pasta, 141
prepping, 14
in recipes, 13
ripening, 8
in salads, 90
  Chopped, 97
  Grapefruit and, 101
  Lettuce, Tomato, and, 98
  Mango and, 109
in salsa, 77
in sandwiches, 124
  Pizza, 128
  Veggie Sub, 129
in soups, 79
  Garden Vegetable, 84
when traveling, 155, 156

B

balsamic vinegar, 197
bamboo sushi mat, 194
  as essential, 12
  when traveling, 154
banana(s)
  Breakfast Pudding, Papaya-, 34
  in desserts
    Ice Cream, Banana, 190
    Malt, Chocolate, 189
    Pudding, Banana, 181
    Pudding, Carob, 182
  freezing, 15
  in fruit salad, 31
  ripening, 8
  Sandwiches, Apple-, 131
  Shake, 188
  in smoothies
    Berry, 28
    green, 41
    Apple-Banana, 39
    Banana-Grape, 47

Creamy Berry, 46
Frosty Banana-Apple, 43
Piña Colada, 29
as snacks, 61
storing, 8
when traveling, 155, 156
bars, 158
Brownies, 166
Basic Green Juice, 23
basics of raw foods, 7–9
basil
  cleaning, 9, 9
  in green smoothies, 38
  Pesto, 78
    Dressing, 119
    Zucchini Pasta al, 139
  in salad dressings
    Goddess, 116
    Pesto, 119
  in side dish, 151
  in soup, 84
batch preparation of recipes, 16
Bean Hummus, Garbanzo, 70
beans, 154. *See also* specific types of
beet(s)
  grater for/grating, 11, 13
  in juices
    Carrot-Celery-Beet, 19
    Fasting, 22
    Pink Apple, 19
  mandoline for, 11
  peeling, 96
  prepping, 14
  in salads
    Rainbow, 96
    Shaved Beet, 110
  as side dish, 143
  spiralizer for, 11
belgian endive, in salad, 111
bell pepper(s). *See also* specific types of
  in salad, 97
  Stuffed, 142
berry(ies). *See also* specific types of

RESOURCES

BOOKS AND VIDEOS

Raw Food Made Easy DVD by Jennifer Cornbleet

This DVD offers step-by-step instruction for many recipes and tips found in *Raw Food Made Easy for 1 or 2 People.*

Raw for Dessert by Jennifer Cornbleet

You can stay vegetarian, vegan, gluten-free, or just plain health-conscious and still eat delicious cakes, candies, cookies, compotes, crumbles, custards, pies, ice creams, and sorbets! In *Raw for Dessert*, Jennifer shares her favorite easy, no-bake recipes.

EDUCATIONAL RESOURCES

Learn Raw Food ▪ learnrawfood.com

Jennifer Cornbleet's website is the complete online companion to this book. It provides access to recipes, online courses, raw-food ingredients and equipment, and a free monthly newsletter. It's also the place to go to find out about Jennifer's upcoming classes and workshops.

The Conscious Health Institute (CHI) ▪ ConsciousHealthInstitute.org

The Conscious Health Institute is a not-for-profit organization whose mission is to educate the public about issues related to health and healing and to empower individuals to take responsibility for their lives and health. A monthly newsletter and online educational courses are available.

Living Light Culinary Arts Institute ▪ rawfoodchef.com

Living Light Culinary Institute offers certification courses in raw culinary arts for individuals, chefs, and teachers. The institute is located in Fort Bragg, California.

HOLISTIC HEALTH PRACTITIONER

Keyvan Golestaneh, MA, LAC ▪ LapisHolisticHealth.com

Keyvan provides a comprehensive natural approach to health that integrates Chinese Medicine, Ayurveda, bioenergetic healing, bodywork, yoga, and herbal therapy. He emphasizes taking responsibility for one's health and life through self-development, dietary and nutritional education, and conscious exercise. Keyvan can work with any health and life problems. He offers consultations, therapy, workshops, and mentorship in person or by appointment via phone and Internet.

Jennifer Cornbleet is a nationally recognized raw-food chef and instructor and a long-time faculty member at Living Light Culinary Institute in California. She lectures and holds classes in the San Francisco Bay area and internationally. Her website, learnrawfood.com, is a comprehensive resource for both online training and raw-food recipes, information, and products.

Learn Raw Food Online
with Jennifer Cornbleet

Going raw gets even easier—and more fun! In an interactive online training called *Ready for Raw*, Jennifer Cornbleet becomes your personal guide. Through step-by-step instruction, videos, live Q&A, and online discussions, she'll share her many tricks for saving time and effort in the kitchen.

Each of the fifteen easy-to-follow sessions includes printable recipes that Jennifer will demonstrate. She'll also help you move beyond simply following her recipes—and reveal the secrets to putting raw ingredients together in ways that please your own taste buds. You'll come away knowing how to stay raw even when facing cravings, special occasions, and other challenges.

In *Ready for Raw* you'll discover how to:

- Adapt to and maintain a high-raw diet.
- Set up your kitchen so it's raw ready.
- Make super smoothies and juices that enhance health and energy.
- Master raw veggie soups, sides, salads, and entrées.
- Prepare raw snacks, treats, and decadent desserts.
- Keep to a budget.
- Stay raw when you're on the go.
- And much, much more.

This training is a comprehensive and affordable culinary journey, connecting you with Jennifer and fellow raw-food enthusiasts in the comfort of your own home. To sample a session of *Ready for Raw*, visit learnrawfood.com.

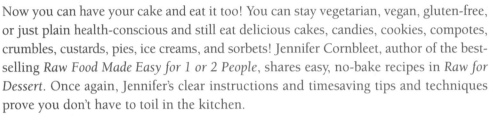

Raw for Dessert
Easy Delights for Everyone

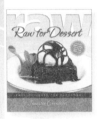

978-1-57067-236-1
$14.95

Now you can have your cake and eat it too! You can stay vegetarian, vegan, gluten-free, or just plain health-conscious and still eat delicious cakes, candies, cookies, compotes, crumbles, custards, pies, ice creams, and sorbets! Jennifer Cornbleet, author of the best-selling *Raw Food Made Easy for 1 or 2 People*, shares easy, no-bake recipes in *Raw for Dessert*. Once again, Jennifer's clear instructions and timesaving tips and techniques prove you don't have to toil in the kitchen.

In *Raw for Dessert* you'll learn how to:

- Avoid white sugar, white flour, dairy products, trans fats, saturated fats, and processed foods.
- Make easy-to-follow recipes, quickly and affordably.
- Prepare a wide variety of scrumptious desserts, including Summer Berry Compote, Caramel Apple Stacks, Crème Brûlée, Pineapple Upside Down Cake, Chocolate Cupcakes, Coconut Cream Pie, Tropical Ambrosia Tart, Pine Nut Caramels, Concord Grape Sorbet, Cookies n' Cream Ice Cream, Knockout Brownie Sundae, and many more.

Raw Food Made Easy DVD

978-1-57067-203-3
$19.95

In her book *Raw Food Made Easy for 1 or 2 People*, Jennifer Cornbleet showed you how to enjoy more fruits, vegetables, and unprocessed whole foods without sacrificing taste. Now, Jennifer's DVD, *Raw Food Made Easy*, can help you take raw to the next level by showing you her techniques, recipes, and strategies:

- Set up your kitchen with basic equipment and staple ingredients.
- Learn how to use a blender, food processor, juicer, knives, and other kitchen tools.
- Make juices, smoothies, and cereals for breakfast.
- Master delicious savory dishes, including soups, pâtés, dressings, and elegant entrées.
- Create beautiful, scrumptious desserts.
- Stay raw while traveling.